AUSTIN-HEALEY 'FROGEYE' SPRITE

Lindsay Porter

CONTENTS

Foulis

Haynes

Titles in the *Super Profile* series

Austin-Healey 'Frogeye' Sprite (F343)

Ferrari 250GTO (F308)

Ford GT40 (F332)

Jaguar D-Type & XKSS (F371)

Jaguar Mk 2 Saloons (F307)

Lotus Elan (F330)

MGB (F305)

Morris Minor & 1000 (ohv) (F331)

Porsche 911 Carrera (F311)

Further titles in this series will be published at
regular intervals. For information on new titles
please contact your bookseller or write to the
publisher.

ISBN 0 85429 343 4

A FOULIS Motoring Book

First published 1983

© **Haynes Publishing Group**

Published by:
Haynes Publishing Group
Sparkford, Yeovil,
Somerset BA22 7JJ

Distributed in USA by:
Haynes Publications Inc.
861 Lawrence Drive, Newbury
Park, California 91320, USA

Editor: Rod Grainger
Dust jacket design: Rowland Smith
Page Layout: Teresa Woodside
Printed in England by: J.H.Haynes &
Co. Ltd

FOREWORD

The Mk I Sprite is no longer a common sight on the open road but should you catch a glimpse of one breezing along on a summer's day, take your eyes off the car if you can and glance at the other passers-by. The smiles they will invariably be wearing will tell you what sort of car the 'Frogeye' (or 'Bugeye') really is. It's cheeky, pert, impetuous and charming, with a character so strong that it's out of all proportion to its size — after all, on the face of it, the 'Frogeye' is hardly what you would call a prime physical specimen! It's far from being powerfully built and indeed its wheels look decidedly skinny by today's standards. Its rear end looks a bit on the heavy side while at the front, its 'eyes' are, well, somewhat protruberant to put it mildly! But somehow, when taken as a whole, the car rises well above its shortcomings; certainly, getting on for fifty thousand buyers thought so when the car was new and nowadays the 'Frogeye' looks set for the sort of cult following and stardom formerly reserved for the T-series M.G. Midgets. Unfortunately, the Mk I Sprite has been through the same phase of worthlessness to which even the Midgets were once prone and through scrapping, its numbers have been reduced. Luckily, thanks to the law of supply and demand, virtually any 'Frogeye' is now worth rebuilding and so restoration components are available to enable even the roughest Mk I Sprite to be rescued. Once restored, the 'Frogeye' must be one of the easiest and cheapest cars to maintain and keep on the road. As the original sales brochure said, *"The car that offers so much ... for so little ..."*

The reader will find that this *Super Profile* is an affectionate, but objective, cameo of the Mark One Sprite from its inception until it was replaced by the Mk II Sprite/Mk I Midget in 1961. Although only a small publication, between these covers will be found a highly detailed and hopefully, well rounded picture of one of Britain's most well loved sports cars.

I would like to take this opportunity to thank all of those people who helped so wholeheartedly in the production of this book: the owners who kindly allowed me to photograph their cars during International Healey Day at the Three-Counties showground, and other venues; my friends Grahame Sykes and Jed Watts at Spridgebits who gave many hours of their time to identifying elusive production change points and provided a great deal of second-to-none practical advice and technical information; *Motor* and *Autocar* magazines kindly allowed us to reproduce their contemporary road tests of 'Frogeye' Sprites — a very valuable addition to this publication.

Thanks are also due to Peter Ablett and James Willis, for making their cars available and to John Wheatley for his help in 'finding' James' car. I would also like to extend my gratitude to the Avoncroft Museum of Buildings, Bromsgrove, near Birmingham for making their facilities freely available.

Lindsay Porter

HISTORY

Family Tree

When, in 1959, the latest offspring of a young but well connected motoring family was born, the status that lay behind the family name was never in any question. The Austin-Healey Sprite (not known as the 'Mk I' of course until the Mk II came along), affectionately dubbed and instantly recognised as the 'Frogeye' Sprite in England and 'Bugeye' in the 'States, had a parentage which combined established respectability and youthful zest in equal parts.

First, the established part. The name 'Austin' derived from that of founder, Herbert Austin, who had become Manager of the Wolseley Sheep Shearing Company in 1883 at the age of 27. He was quick to see the potential of motor cars and he had true Wolseley series production under way by 1900. However, in 1905, Austin quarrelled with his fellow Wolseley directors and left to form his own company, manufacturing cars under his own name. Even up to 1941, when Austin died, at the age of 74, he was still in charge and still very much in harness. During his lifetime, the Austin marque developed a reputation for the honest dependability and a rejection of newness for its own

sake. For instance, Austin were the last manufacturers in England to stop fitting windscreens that sat bolt upright and to replace them with the 'modern' sloping-back variety! Although prodigious numbers of different models were built, one Austin above all was to leave its mark indelibly upon the motoring scene. It was known as the Austin Seven and it began life with a tiny 696cc engine, quickly upped a little to 747cc. Its enormous appeal which lasted right through times of great recession, was based on reliability, simplicity of construction and low cost. The uncluttered A-frame chassis was fitted with only a folding canvas top at first but a wide variety of body styles were to be offered over the years. The engine was smooth by comparison with its competitors, all of them rough-running twin cylinder jobs, while the Seven's engine was an in-line four.

The tiny Sevens were the last of a line of Austin racers to take to the track. Austin the man had never shown a great interest in motor sport but there is no doubt that he recognised its commercial significance as a way of publicising his cars. His first racer had been a 9.7-litre six-cylinder Grand Prix model of 1908 and other racing cars came and went but it was not until the 1930s that the Austin Company began to take a serious interest in racing. The car they chose was, almost inevitably, the Austin 7. 1930 was the best year for track successes, with one of the works cars achieving a splendid victory on handicap at the Brooklands racetrack with an average speed of over 83 miles per hour. The 1939 successes had the effect of creating intense competition with a relative newcomer to the scene, a firm by the name of M.G. ...

In 1933, a most extraordinary Austin 7 racer, still with a side-valve engine, achieved the startling speed of 113mph (and won back three records from M.G. in the process) but in so doing convinced

the Austin management that the side-valve engine's natural limit had been found. While some Austin 7 racers were fitted with side-valve engines and superchargers from 1934, others went way beyond the original concept in being fitted with twin overhead camshaft engines. From this point on, Austin's participation in motor sport became less eventful until, after Herbert Austin's death and the elevation of his successor, Leonard Lord, Austin's involvement in motorsport drew to a complete halt. A side-effect of Austin's interest in motor sport, and one which is most relevant to this story, is that the company exploited the interest aroused in the Austin Seven racers by producing sporting models of their own. The Austin Seven Nippy and the Ulster as well as those fitted with sporting bodies by coach builders such as S.S. (later to become Jaguar) were the nearest equivalents to Austin's postwar sports car range, a range that they would develop in collaboration with the Healey concern.

By comparison with the Austin tradition the Healey family's motoring involvement was young, or at least far less well known. On the other hand, the Healey half of the double-barrel name had a genuinely family feel to it. The Donald Healey Motor Company Ltd was based at Warwick, England, and was headed by Donald Healey and his sons Geoffrey and Brian. In the 1930s, following his 1931 success as overall winner of the Monte Carlo Rally in an Invicta, Donald Healey held the position of Technical Director at Triumph where he had been responsible for the development of the Gloria and the Dolomite. In 1939 he became the firm's General Manager but after the war, Triumph ceased to exist as an independent concern and so Healey began to build motor cars on his own account, the first being announced in 1946. Typically, his cars consisted of a separate chassis with a form of trailing link front suspension which was highly expensive to produce, quite superb in concept, but prone to giving trouble. They were fitted with 2-litre Riley engines and four-speed Riley gearboxes but they came with a variety of body styles and types such as the Warwick, Elliott, Duncan, Sportsmobile, Silverstone, Tickford and Abbott: the Silverstone being the most famous, because of its competition successes.

The Healey concern was always tiny and under-financed (which is why it had to look outside for its power trains) but gained for itself an enviable reputation on both sides of the Atlantic. The cars were always carefully shaped and lightweight and consequently were capable of high performance. Also there was an air of engineering integrity about them from the chassis frame, designed by Donald's son Geoffrey, through to that front suspension, which was highly effective when in good order.

By 1949 as the supply of Riley engines dried up, the Healey concern was able to strike a deal with the Nash Kelvinator Corporation in America following a chance shipboard meeting between Donald Healey and George W. Mason, Nash's President, whereby a Healey chassis was fitted with a Nash 6-cylinder, 3.8-litre engine and a body whose front and rear wing styling was to be repeated on the bodywork of more famous Healeys still to come. It was embellished with a Nash grille, bumpers and other fixtures and fittings. The Nash-Healey was sold only in the United States (although the rare Alvis-Healey appeared in great Britain sharing the Nash-Healey's body) and was a modest success in sales terms. More importantly, it taught the Healeys that co-ordination with a much larger concern was not only desirable but necessary if real expansion was to take place.

The breakthrough for Healey came at the time of the 1952 Earls Court Motor Show. The Healey 100 was completed immediately prior to the show's opening. The grille, designer Gerry Coker was later to recall, was a disappointment to all concerned. He continued, ''It was at this point that the late Sir Leonard Lord made his manufacturing proposal, and I in turn was requested to redesign the badge to incorporate the Austin name. We then had an *Austin* Healey 100 on the stand within two days of the show opening.''

Sir Leonard Lord had taken over as Chairman at Longbridge within a year of the death of Austin. Indeed he had been appointed by Austin as works director in 1938 and was obviously groomed by Lord Austin (as he had then become) to be his successor, a role for which he was eminently suited. Leonard Lord was known as a volatile, ambitious man with the ability to make sound snap decisions and an absolute determination to see them put into practice. It was thus typical of Lord that he should enter into a deal with Donald Healey after only the briefest consideration and that the decision should prove such a wise one. The two men clearly held each other in some respect and it was as the result of one of their meetings in the winter of 1956 that the concept of the 'Frogeye' Sprite was born. As Geoffrey Healey writes in his book, *More Healeys:*

''In his blunt, down to earth manner, Len Lord then commented that what we needed was a small, low cost sports car to fill the gap left by the disappearance of the Austin 7 Nippy and Ulster models of pre-war fame. What he would really like to see, he said, was a bug. It is impossible to tell whether he was simply thinking aloud, or deliberately giving DMH (Donald Healey) a broad hint of what we should do, but this conversation certainly set DMH thinking as he drove back from Longbridge.''

In 1956, Healey's body designer was Gerry Coker, who was to write several years later in a letter to the Austin Healey Owners' Club: ''For 1956 Mr Healey wanted a cheap two-seater, that a chap could keep in his bike shed'. The original design had concealed headlamps and I liked to think of it as the poor kid's Ferrari. When I left the company in January of 1957 the bodyshell was finished, and I thought it looked pretty good. Unfortunately, it did not appear in production as I had hoped, though it seemed to enjoy production as a frog-eyed Sprite.''

So perhaps Geoffrey Healey's implied connection between Leonard Lord's use of the word ''bug'' and the car's subsequent bug-like appearance is one of those cases where the memory's rear-view mirror has become a little misty. Even so, it's a nice thought!

A third area of influence and one that can be easily overlooked, is that of M.G. Although M.G. have not featured in the story so far, save as competitors during Austin's relatively brief burst of activity in motorsport, when the Sprite did gain production status it was at Abingdon that the car was built and it could even be argued that it was an Abingdon heritage that was being reincarnated. It is certain that the Healey concern had no experience of small sports cars, other than their relatively crude prototypes. The Austin experience too, as has been shown, was one which was connected with 'sensible' family motoring to such an extent that its sporting connections were almost an aberration. On the other hand, M.G. were, quite simply ... M.G.!

The immediately pre- and postwar years had seen the M.G. success story founded largely upon the sales of small, lightweight sports cars, as robust as they were rudimentary and known as M.G. Midgets. M-, J-, then PA-Midgets were derived, ironically, from another 'ordinary' small car (albeit with an overhead camshaft engine), the first Morris Minor, with half elliptic springing front and rear and a capacity of 847cc. The theme struck a chord with enthusiasts in such a way that postwar sales of the little Midgets, by then in TD and TF forms, took off, especially in the United States. However, early in 1955, M.G. chose to replace the TF, itself powered by a 1466cc unit by the time of its demise, with the MGA which, though hugely successful in its own right, left a gap in the market for small sports cars which Len Lord of Austin, and Donald Healey set about filling.

The origins of the double-barrel surname have been explored and the appropriateness of the fact that the new car was to be assembled at Abingdon has been touched upon. Only the background to the new car's name has to be explained. Geoffrey Healey commented that the prototypes were given the designation numbers "Q1" and "Q2" while the prototypes' nickname was "The Tiddler". Donald Healey himself chose the name "Sprite", although it had of course been used before by Riley. The title to the name was vested in Daimler, however inappropriate that may now seem, and one can imagine that it would not have been too difficult to persuade them to relinquish the name!

Concept

The idea of a cheap two-seater "that a chap could keep in his bicycle shed" is something that is very well established in British sports-car lore but it has seldom been achieved with complete success The 1930s-on M.G. Midgets, the pre-war Austin Seven sports, the Triumph Spitfire and the brave but ill-fated little Berkeleys are perhaps the only others to come close to matching the Sprite, but it is arguable that none ever surpassed it. In being able to lay claim to the excellent 948cc A-series Austin engine and gearbox and the Austin A35's front suspension and rear axle, as well as the Morris Minor steering rack, the Sprite was based on mechanical foundations which were as sound

as any could be; ubiquitous enough to make their unit price as low as possible and yet eminently suitable for tuning and development whilst still retaining utter reliability. Around these keystones, the Healey genius for instinctive engineering and perceptive marketing flair produced a superb package. By keeping brightwork to a minimum, making use of a spartan though fairly comfortable cockpit, doing without a bootlid (in its place substituting a stressed rear panel), and by the use of chassis-less, unitary construction, it was possible to produce a practical package while keeping the price right down. Rear suspension was by quarter-elliptics, giving positive, almost faultless roadholding and the whole front end bodywork lifted up as a unit providing superb access to all components except the battery. Rejected along the design and development path were Gerry Coker's pop-up headlamps, which would have added greatly to the cost but which also would have added a note of unwarranted sophistication. As it was, the Sprite was easily able to undercut all of the opposition at a U.K. price of only £690 including Purchase Tax in May 1958. At the same time, the Austin-Healey Hundred Six cost £1,329, the MGA cost £1,013, the Triumph TR3A cost £1,065 and only the diminutive and somewhat unreliable Berkeley was cheaper at £500, but with a 328cc engine, no dealership network and no comparisons to be made in terms of reliability or performance. There was never any real competition!

Design

Following their collaboration over the Austin-Healey 100, the Healey concern had received increasing assistance from Austin in the development of a new, small sports car. They received working drawings, supplied by Austin's Geoff Cooper and actual components for use in prototype

development. Among the Austin A35 components supplied to Healeys was included the car's fairly orthodox front suspension with a single, pressed steel lower wishbone, coil springs, and upper links formed by the Armstrong shock absorber lever arms.

The A35 engine had first seen service in 1951 in the Austin A30 and was essentially a smaller version of the 1200cc Austin A40 unit which was later to find fame in an enlarged form in the MGA and MGB. The smaller A-series engine, as it was to become known, was originally of 803cc capacity and was a conventional four-cylinder with a three bearing crankshaft running in thin-wall bearings, the first British production engine to do so. One of its most notable features was its highly efficient cylinder head designed by Harry Weslake, an independent consultant who discovered that a heart-shaped combustion area with a protruding peninsula between inlet and exhaust valves permitted gases to swirl and so promoted complete and efficient combustion of the mixture. The engine was used in the Morris Minor from 1952 and was subsequently enlarged to 948cc and used in both Austin and Morris small cars from 1956. Actually, the engine was redeveloped rather than simply enlarged, its bores being siamesed (ie: losing the water jackets that were previously situated between them) and lead-indium bearings were accompanied by great improvements in crankshaft and connecting rod strength and bearing sizes. These alterations were highly significant in that they allowed sufficient reserves of strength for subsequent Austin-Healey Sprite engine uprating and for the large amount of additional tuning which many private owners were to carry out. In short, the engine was almost unburstable.

In its basic A35 form and fitted with a Zenith carburettor, the engine was somewhat underpowered for use in a sports car, developing only 34bhp. Even the Minor engine equipped with an S.U. carburettor developed 37bhp and so, by the simple expedient of installing twin $1\frac{1}{8}$ inch SUs the power was raised to 43bhp at 5200rpm. At the same time stronger valve springs were fitted along with stellite faced exhaust valve seats and copper-indium become the material used for main as well as big end bearings. Stronger clutch springs were also fitted. The standard compression ratio remained, at 8.3 to 1, and although the Sprite engine's performance was perhaps less than breathtaking, plenty of scope remained for tuning while retaining reliability.

An MGA-style single-reservoir, twin-cylinder clutch and brake master cylinder was used giving a hydraulically operated clutch and brakes (Lockheed). The standard A35 gearbox was retained (with a rather large 'gap' between second and third gears), along with the standard 4.22 to 1 axle ratio. The use of hydraulically operated brakes meant that the A35's operating mechanism, which dangled below the rear axle, could be dispensed with and Minor-type brakes could be fitted, with the handbrake mechanism operating through the wheel cylinders.

This mechanical effort had been preceded by much design work on the construction and shape of the car. Austin's own 1953 ideas for a tubular-framed sports car with styling similarities to the A40 Sports produced by Jensen Motors, were never considered or indeed, seen by the Healeys. Instead, the Sprite was to be an altogether more exciting package and in fact became the country's first unitary construction sports car. Geoff Healey designed a floorpan which was in effect a tray with hollow sills and rear panel and a sturdy scuttle. All the car's suspension loadings were fed into this central area; front loads came back into the bulkhead via forward facing 'chassis' legs and, amazingly for a low cost car,

rear loadings were fed forwards into the rear floor/rear panel area through quarter-elliptic springs, in the style of the much more expensive and sophisticated Jaguar Mk I, which was already in production. Unlike the more conventional half-elliptic springs which are located at each end quarter-elliptics are held by the bodyframe only at one end with the axle mounted at the other; thus a great deal of force has to be absorbed through the springs' bodyframe location points. The Sprite's springs were located in boxes let into the double rear panel and were reinforced by a plate running under the floor which itself was strengthened by a channel section spot-welded to the top of the floor, in line with the springs.

This punt-type floorpan, complete with boot floor and front inner wings, was manufactured by John Thompson Motor Pressings Ltd of Wolverhampton, the two prototype floorpans being built by them for a nominal £50 and the quotation for the production pressed and spot-welded floorpans coming to the grand sum of £12-10s-0d each. In fact Thompsons, who had spare capacity at the time and were keen to gain the work, underestimated their own costs and began by making a substantial loss on every one of the flimsy looking frames produced — at least they *looked* flimsy in comparison with the 'Big' Healey chassis which Thompsons produced in the same factory. (The author can well remember being shown round the shop floor by one of the old hands who took a half-finished Sprite floor pan and shook it disdainfully making it flex and 'crash' like a wobble board.)

An indication of the instinctive nature of car design in the '50s compared to today's world of computers and robotics, is given by Geoffrey Healey's own account of the next stage in the process from his book, *More Healeys*.

''We attempted to use the A35's steering gear but it quickly

became obvious that little of the Austin stuff would suit. Instead, we took the Morris Minor rack and pinion and laid this in position. Once we had determined the correct position and checked that the steering geometry was good through the various wheel movements, we had to get some special steering arms made up. Jack Merralls, our Warwick blacksmith, made us a pair in EN16 steel which were then heat treated by the local gasworks. These were then filed to the finished shape, drilled and fitted.''

So it was that a large part of the Sprite's distinctive character, its beautifully responsive steering, came about by the combination of chance and the typical Healey brilliance for instinctive engineering.

In order to complete the first running chassis, the twin carburettors were fitted in conjunction with a manifold that was 'cut and shut' from an existing M.G. part and later, after the very earliest stages in road testing, Panel Craft bodywork and Lucas electrics were fitted. The installation of a rev counter was found to be difficult. The usual place for its connection, at the rear of the camshaft, was already spoken for by the A-series engine's oil pump. Between them Lucas and Smith came to the rescue, designing a gearbox to fit on the rear of the Lucas generator to drive the Smiths tachometer at the correct speed via a cable drive.

A major feature of the prototypes which was lacking on production cars was the retracting headlamps, their lenses facing skywards in the manner of certain modern Porsches. This Gerry Coker feature had to be dropped partly because of cost and partly because of the complexity of providing a linkage that operated in conjunction with the one-piece lift-open bonnet. After the Sprite was given approval by the BMC hierarchy the final stages in the design process were begun. At this point Gerry Coker left Healeys to work in America and Les Ireland took over as body engineer, before long replacing the prototype's crude-looking door hinges by hidden internal ones that were actually cheaper to produce. Eddie Maher and his team at Morris Motors engine department had already carried out their engine modifications when production schedules were set out. John Thompson's chassis frames would travel from Wolverhampton to Swindon where Pressed Steel would fabricate the bodies and spot-weld them in place. From there the shells would travel to Cowley to be painted and finally to Abingdon where final assembly would take place, the whole round trip forming a 'production line' of around 150 miles in length! Longbridge, incidentally, which would have seemed the natural home for an Austin, was ruled out as the production venue because it was only possible there to insert engines from beneath the production line track, a feat which was impossible on the Sprite because of the nature of its construction. Consequently, versatile old Abingdon found themselves with yet another non-M.G. to produce, but at least it was a sports car and a fine one at that. And before long, Sid Enever and his Abingdon team were to leave their mark on the design of the Mk I's successor.

Production Modifications

Although one fewer than 49,000 'Frogeye' sprites were built, production changes during the life of the car were very few in number. At very early stages, the interior door handles shrank a little in length and sprouted a chrome knob and the hood to windscreen frame fitting was altered. Earlier cars' hoods had been held at the front by a row of nine lift-the-dot fasteners lined up along the top of the windscreen frame. The main

shortcoming of this system was that rain was forced under the hood to an extent unacceptable even to hardened sports car enthusiasts of the era and an alternative fitting system was introduced as early as October 1958. The improved fixing method consisted of a narrow pocket across the front of the hood into which a length of flat steel was inserted. The windscreen frame was made with a downwards facing slot along its top edge instead of the earlier fasteners, and the pocket, stiffened with the steel bar was pushed upwards into the slot and held there by the tension in the hood.

Towards the end of the summer of 1959, a Sprite fitted with a hardtop (supplied by the Donald Healey Motor Company) became available along with Weathershields Ltd sliding panel side-screens, fitted as standard in place of the usual one-piece items. The interior of the hardtop was of a rather austere, bare fibreglass finish but it made the car much more snug inside. However, while *The Autocar* reported that "draughts are eliminated almost completely and there is no leakage in heavy rain" they also went on to say that the car became considerably noisier with the hardtop fitted. The hugely improved side-screens became available as an optional extra, at the same time as the introduction of the hardtop, at a cost of £3.15s plus Purchase Tax but including an allowance for the non-use of the basic flimsy side-screens. In fact it is suspected that the improved side-screens were another of those theoretical options; in practice they were fitted whether wanted or not and were probably a device for improving the car while keeping the basic list price as low as possible. This theory would certainly help to account for the extreme rarity of the original one-piece side-screens today.

At their Warwick headquarters, the Healey company were constantly in the throes of new model development, some of it

prompted by B.M.C. most of it purely in-house and, seemingly, almost for the hell of it. One such project was the 'Super Sprite' which was begun as early as 1959. A dramatically more powerful 1100cc Coventry Climax engine was fitted (the same unit to be found in the then contemporary Lotus Elite) and a Les Ireland design of alloy body was fitted with a deep swage line sweeping from front to rear proclaiming its status as a Healey. The car was very much faster than the standard Sprite (a Brabham converted 1962 M.G. Midget with similar Climax engine had a theoretical maximum of around 112mph) and was fitted with disc brakes all round. Although the car must have seemed most exciting at the time, the response it drew from B.M.C. was less than wholehearted – they even went so far as to issue a stern warning that 'outside' engines were not to be used again!

Undeterred, Healeys went on to produce a range of alternative Sprites which reached various stages of development. In the end, the variation on the theme that turned the car into the Mk II was brought about on B.M.C.'s instigation. The circumstances surrounding the lead up to the new car can be seen to enter the realms of farce when it is realised that the Healeys were told to redevelop the car's front end while Sid Enever at Abingdon was told to get on with redesigning the rear end – and the two were specifically told not to communicate with one another! Of course, with only an hour's drive between the two concerns, each quickly found out what the other was doing and they were able to collaborate. The Sprite's happy looking front end was replaced at Warwick, at first by one which placed the headlamps in the wings but retained the characterful grille, but later that too was changed. Abingdon squared-up the rear end in a way which was soon to be seen again on the MGB and a boot lid was added. The suspension system however, remained the same for the time being.

The Mk I Sprite was such an individualistic little car that it was no surprise that owners tended to be those who prized individuality. While B.M.C. continued to market virtually the same package 48, 999 times over, the cars' owners gladly took advantage of the tuning 'goodies' available through a wide variety of suppliers. These ranged from cheap but non-sensical economy devices, that failed to work, right through to superchargers, with a wide range of offerings in between. The most suitable modifications were those developed by Healeys themselves.

The justifiably famous special-bodied Targa Florio Sprite was foreshadowed by the Mk I Sprite which was run in the 1959 Targa Florio with tuned engine and general rally preparation but without any alterations to the bodywork save an opened-up grille to give a little extra cooling. In the event, the dramatically altered Targa Florio cars were not introduced until 1964. Strangely, not all the Warwick modifications then available were used on this first Targa Florio car. In April 1959, *The Motor* reported on a Warwick tuned Sprite with engine modified to Stage 4 and with disc brakes and wire wheels. A closer ratio gearbox was also fitted (it was discontinued for a while but later re-introduced, eventually being introduced as standard to the Mk II) and a twin exhaust system. *The Motor* felt that the front anti-roll bar and wider track imparted by the wire wheel conversion made a significant difference to handling and they reported that, in spite of being heavier than standard, the little car was capable of over 90mph — an impressive speed for 1959 — but the cost was not low. On top of the Sprite's basic £631, the cost of improvements added just over £166 for the parts alone, without allowing for the cost of fitting and thus added more than 25% to the cost of the car. The price of individuality!

Motorsport

Frankly, the Mk I Sprite was never overwhelmingly successful in international motorsport: simply, it was too small. That, however, didn't stop folk having a go!

In 1959 the factory took one of their high speed record cars (although they were scarcely recognisable as cars at all, having been designed to be as 'slippery' as possible) to Utah salt flats fitted with a 948cc engine. They called it an Austin-Healey Sprite and it took International Class G records to an average 145.56 mph over 50 kilometres. Racing and rallying successes were quickly to follow for cars that were more recognisably Sprites with 1st, 2nd and 3rd in class in the 1959 Alpine Rally, and a class win for a private entrant in the Leinster Trophy at the Dundrod racetrack in Ireland. These initial successes were not to be followed up with any consistency. Although there were a number of class wins in a variety of events and the cars were driven by drivers as illustrious as Stirling Moss, their impact was not made best use of by B.M.C.'s publicity department and it was, after all, difficult to make the right sort of impact with class wins when other members of the manufacturer's stable were capable of and were gaining outright victories in a variety of theatres of battle.

Nowadays, early Sprites are more successful than they ever were in their heyday in competitions more suited to their abilities. In British Modsport and Prodsport races, Sprites are given the chance to shine and they achieve similar distinction in their classes, 'Stateside. They are still seen in that eccentric British sport known alternatively as Trials events or "Mudplugging", and, in Autotests, where all round visibility and precision steering are the greatest assets in driving round obstacles and into and through 'gates', they can be almost invincible. In providing enjoyment for the impecunious, there's *still* nothing to beat them!

Reasons for Discontinuation

The Mk I Sprite did not so much cease production as evolve into the Mk II Sprite/Mk I Midget. The reasons were straightforward and were far short of an indictment of the earlier car. In those days, comments on the Sprite's front end were mixed, so it was decided to replace it with a conventional front end. The lack of a proper opening boot could be annoying and the provision of a lid was a logical step. Commercially, the move made a lot of sense. The M.G. name has always had the sort of status that the manufacturer could exploit to good effect on the right car and, moreover, the 'Frogeye's' sales had begun to fall. Although, ironically, sales actually fell further immediately after the change, it was a change that had looked inevitable.

EVOLUTION

The **Chassis Number** (or **Car Number**) is stamped on a plate secured to the left-hand inner wheel arch valance under the bonnet. The **Engine Number** is stamped on a plate secured to the right-hand side of the cylinder block above the dynamo.

The Chassis, or Car Number consists of a code which presents the following information:

1st character indicates make (H = Healey)
2nd character indicates engine type A = A-series engine)
3rd character indicates the factory code for body type (N = 2-seater tourer)
4th number indicates series (the Sprite was the fifth in the Austin-Healey series, from the factory's point of view)

Production modifications

Chassis numbers quoted here are what manufacturers know as 'pure' chassis numbers (ie **all** cars built after the number shown are fitted with those parts which relate to the chassis number change point). However, it may well be that, because of production line supply techniques, some cars which

appear before the given change point will be fitted with 'later' parts.

The Sprite MkI is notable for having had an exceptionally small number of production modifications. Many of those shown here are minor in nature and nearly all took place within the first six months of the model's life.

Chassis No. H-AN5 501: March 31, 1958, production began. May 20th 1958, Austin-Healey Sprite announced.
Options: UK May 1958: heater £20.16s.3d; radio £25.0s.0d; tachometer £4.10s.0d; front bumper and over-riders £6.0s.0d; screenwasher £2.5s.0d; 6-ply tyres £7.2s.6d; laminated windscreen £4.2s.6d; fresh air unit £6.0s.0d; tonneau cover £6.0s.0d. (NB: tachometer and heater were probably 'theoretical' options in that they were fitted before delivery except in the case of export cars intended for warmer countries where heaters were more often not fitted. In this way, it is surmised, advertised prices could be kept as low as possible.)

H-AN5 946: Gearbox synchro. assembly improved.
H-AN5 1073: Thermostat type changed.
H-AN5 1397: Inlet and exhaust valves – modified type fitted.
H-AN5 1551: Carb. fuel chamber lids modified.
H-AN5 1606: Sidescreen mounting brackets, fixing screws and door top finishers modified.
H-AN5 3444: Tachometer cable improved.
H-AN5 3689: Speedometer cable improved.
H-AN5 4333: Rear axle case slightly modified in conjunction with altered radius arm mounting bracket, incorporating shock absorber mounting points for extra

location. Shock absorber assembly modified accordingly.
H-AN5 4695: Under-bonnet air intake shape modified.
H-AN5 4800: Steering arm fixing bolts reduced in number from two to one per side.
H-AN5 4996: Clutch pedal modified.
H-AN5 5321: Ferrule–blanking tool hole in rear crossmember fitted.
H-AN5 5477: October 16, 1958 nine-stud hood-to-screen top fixing changed to slot-in type of screen fixing.
H-AN5 10344: Door handles (interior) shortened and chome plated knobs added at their ends and the latches improved. Rear wheel arch chassis rails strengthened and reinforced. Windscreen side stanchions and hood front panel modified at same time.
Late 1959/Early 1960: Hardtop model introduced with Warwick-designed glass reinforced plastic hardtop as standard and with modified sidescreens built by Weathershields Ltd in place of one-piece lightweight sidescreens. Weathershields sidescreens incorporate two-piece Perspex (Plexiglas) panels, the rear of which slide open. (NB: It is suspected these improved sidescreens became another 'theoretical' optional extra in that they were listed as such but were probably fitted to the cars prior to delivery.)
H-AN5 34558: March 1960, sliding sidescreens were catalogued as standard.
H-AN5 50116: Very early 1961, production ended.

SPECIFICATION

Type designation Austin-Healey Sprite developed under Austin Drawing Office number A.D.O.13. Later known as Austin-Healey Sprite Mk I.

Built Abingdon, England from March 31, 1958 to 1961. Also built from knock-down kits in Sydney, Australia until mid-1962.

Engine BMC A-series unit as used in Morris Minor/Austin A35 except for twin HSl ($1\frac{1}{8}$ in) SU carburettors set at a slight angle from the horizontal and with individual 'pancake' type air filters, special valve springs. Stellited exhaust valve seats and copper-lead main and big-end bearings. Cast iron block and head, pressed steel sump, 4-cylinder in-line, overhead valve with pushrods, camshaft in block. Capacity 948cc (57.87cu.in) Bore & Stroke 62.9x76.2mm (2.48x30in).
Maximum power: 43bhp (nett) at 5000rpm.
Maximum torque (nett): 52lb/ft at 3300rpm
Maximum bmep (nett): 136lb/sq.in at 3000rpm.
Fuel pump: A.C. mechanical type, mounted in side of block and driven by camshaft.
Sump capacity: $6\frac{7}{8}$ Imp pints (3.34 litres)

Transmission Rear wheel drive from front mounted engine. Four speed gearbox bolted to rear engine plate.
Synchromesh available on top three ratios.
Overall gear ratios: Top, 4.22; 3rd, 5.96; 2nd, 10.02; 1st, 15.31. Final drive, 4.22 to 1.
Reverse 19.68 Hypoid bevel rear axle. Clutch of Borg and Beck manufacture, $6\frac{1}{4}$in diameter, hydraulic operation.

Chassis frame and bodywork 2-door, 2-seater convertible of all-steel unitary (chassisless) construction. Floorpan pressed and constructed at John Thompson Motor Pressings Ltd in Wolverhampton, England with sills of 0.048in (1.22mm) thickness.
A substantial front scuttle receives front end loadings and comprises a central, vertical box running almost from scuttle top to floor into which the gearbox body protrudes and each side of which are driver's and passenger's footwells. The battery and heater shelf forms the top face of the box as seen from inside the engine compartment. Protruding forward from the scuttle are 'chassis' legs, tied together at their forward end by

a box-section crossmember.

The one-piece floor (the propeller shaft runs above it, inside the transmission tunnel) proceeds back from a floor-level crossmember parallel with the scuttle/dashboard top to a shallow rear bulkhead and is supported by the deep transmission tunnel, 2-piece sills and a box section running front-to-rear in line with the rear springs and mounted on top of the floor. Rear spring loadings are taken forward into a hollow rear bulkhead of triangular section and the floor/box section already described. Other body panels, including the stressed rear panel, were produced and fitted at the Pressed Steel Company, Swindon. Bodyshell rust inhibited, and painted, at the Morris works at Cowley.

Wheelbase: 6ft 8in (203cm).

Track: front 3ft 9¾in (116cm).
       rear: 3ft 8¾in (114cm).

Overall length: (without front bumper) 11ft 0⅝in (337cm), (with front bumper) 11ft 5¼in (349cm).

Overall width: 4ft 5in (135cm).

Overall height: 4ft 1¾in (126cm) but 3ft 8⅛in (112cm) with hood down.

Ground clearance: 5in (13cm).

Turning circle: right: 31ft 2½in (9.5m).
        left: 32ft 1½in (9.8m).

Kerb weight: 1328lb (602kg).

Weight distribution: 55% front/45% rear.

Fuel tank capacity: 6 Imp. gallons/27.3 litres/7.2 U.S. gallons.

Suspension

Front: Standard Austin A35 coil spring and wishbone components in conjunction with Armstrong lever-type shock absorbers which also act as upper arms of the wishbone assembly.

Rear: Quarter-elliptic 15-leaf springs with 16 inch free length between mounting bracket and axle. Upper torque links fabricated from channel pressings run above, and parallel to, the springs. Rubber bump stops and canvas rebound straps.

Steering

Morris Minor-type steering rack giving 2½ turns from lock-to-lock.

Brakes

Conventional Lockheed hydraulic system with M.G.-type shared brake and clutch master cylinder.

Front: 7in drum with twin leading 1³⁄₁₆in wide shoes.

Rear: 7in drum with leading-and-trailing 1³⁄₁₆in wide shoes.

Handbrake operated by cable and rod, with its compensating gear attached to the axle casing.

Wheels and Tyres

Ventilated pressed steel disc wheels, 4 studs 13 x 3½in. 5.20 x 13in tubeless tyres.

Tyre pressures: 18psi front: 20psi rear.

Electrical system

12 volt 43 amp hour battery mounted ahead of the scuttle. Positive earth Lucas dynamo (with integral mechanical tachometer drive mounted at its rear) and Lucas voltage regulator. Lucas coil ignition and wiring harness made up to standard Lucas colour coding scheme. 2 fuses, non-cancelling direction indicators (white front, amber rear), self-parking windscreen wipers.

Performance

Maximum speed 81mph

Speed in gears: 3rd gear 65mph, 2nd gear 38mph, 1st gear 23 mph

Acceleration: 0-50mph, 13.4 secs; 0-60mph, 20.5 secs.

Standing quarter-mile: 21.2 secs

Acceleration in gears:
Top: 20-40mph, 12.6 secs; 40-60mph, 14.5 secs.
Third: 20-40mph. 7.8 secs; 40-60mph 14.5 secs.
Fuel consumption: Driven hard, 33 miles per Imperial gallon. Touring, 44 miles per Imperial gallon.

May 21, 1958

ROAD TESTS

600

The Motor Road Test No. 15/58

Make: Austin-Healey   **Type:** Sprite

Makers: Austin Motor Co. Ltd., Longbridge, Birmingham.

Test Data

CONDITIONS: Weather : Warm and dry with moderate breeze. (Temperature 70°—74°F., Barometer: 30.2—30.4 in Hg.). Surface: Dry tarred macadam. Fuel : Premium-grade pump petrol (Approx. 95 Research Method Octane Rating).

INSTRUMENTS
Speedometer at 30 m.p.h.	3% fast
Speedometer at 60 m.p.h.	5% fast
Speedometer at 80 m.p.h.	8% fast
Distance recorder	2% fast

WEIGHT
Kerb weight (unladen, but with oil, coolant and fuel for approx. 50 miles) .. .. .. 12¼ cwt.
Front/rear distribution of kerb weight .. 55/45
Weight laden as tested .. .. .. 16 cwt.

MAXIMUM SPEEDS
Flying Quarter Mile
Mean of four opposite runs .. .. 82.9 m.p.h.
Best one-way time equals .. .. 86.5 m.p.h.

"Maximile" Speed (Timed quarter mile after one mile accelerating from rest).
Mean of four opposite runs .. .. 81.1 m.p.h.
Best one-way time equals .. .. 83.3 m.p.h.

Speed in Gears (at 6,000 r.p.m.).
Max. speed in 3rd gear .. .. 65 m.p.h.
Max. speed in 2nd gear .. .. 39 m.p.h.
Max. speed in 1st gear .. .. 25 m.p.h.

FUEL CONSUMPTION
52.5 m.p.g. at constant 30 m.p.h. on level.
54.5 m.p.g. at constant 40 m.p.h. on level.
53.5 m.p.g. at constant 50 m.p.h. on level.
38.0 m.p.g. at constant 60 m.p.h. on level.
36.0 m.p.g. at constant 70 m.p.h. on level.

Overall Fuel Consumption for 1,696 miles, 50.5 gallons, equals 33.6 m.p.g. (8.4 litres/100 km.)

Touring Fuel Consumption (m.p.g. at steady speed midway between 30 m.p.h. and maximum, less 5% allowance for acceleration) 43.0 m.p.g.
Fuel tank capacity (maker's figure) .. 6 gallons

STEERING
Turning circle between kerbs :
Left .. .. 28½ feet
Right .. .. 29½ feet
Turns of steering wheel from lock to lock 2⅓

BRAKES from 30 m.p.h.
0.97 g retardation (equivalent to 31 ft. stopping distance) with 90 lb. pedal pressure.
0.75 g retardation (equivalent to 40 ft. stopping distance) with 75 lb. pedal pressure.
0.49 g retardation (equivalent to 61½ ft. stopping distance) with 50 lb. pedal pressure.
0.22 g retardation (equivalent to 137 ft. stopping distance) with 25 lb. pedal pressure.

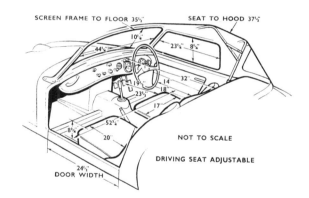

ACCELERATION TIMES from standstill
0-30 m.p.h.	5.1 sec.
0-40 m.p.h.	8.5 sec.
0-50 m.p.h.	13.7 sec.
0-60 m.p.h.	20.5 sec.
0-70 m.p.h.	31.1 sec.
Standing quarter mile	21.8 sec.

ACCELERATION TIMES on Upper Ratios
	Top gear	3rd gear
10-30 m.p.h.	13.7 sec.	8.6 sec.
20-40 m.p.h.	12.6 sec.	7.7 sec.
30-50 m.p.h.	12.6 sec.	8.6 sec.
40-60 m.p.h.	14.4 sec.	11.4 sec.
50-70 m.p.h.	18.5 sec.	—

HILL CLIMBING at sustained steady speeds.
Max. gradient on top gear .. .. 1 in 11.7 (Tapley 190 lb./ton)
Max. gradient on 3rd gear .. .. 1 in 7.5 (Tapley 295 lb./ton)
Max. gradient on 2nd gear .. .. 1 in 4.5 (Tapley 485 lb./ton)

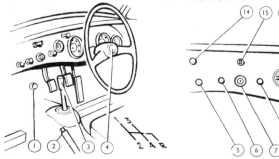

1, Headlamp dip switch. 2, Handbrake. 3, Gear lever. 4, Horn button. 5, Windscreen washers button. 6, Windscreen wipers control. 7, Ignition and lights switch. 8, Heater control. 9, Water thermometer. 10, Headlamp high-beam indicator lamp. 11, Dynamo charge warning lamp. 12, Panel light switch. 13, Trip resetting knob. 14, Choke control. 15, Direction indicator switch. 16, Oil pressure gauge. 17, Starter switch. 18, Tachometer. 19, Direction indicator warning lamp. 20, Speedometer and distance recorder. 21, Fuel contents gauge.

B18

The Austin-Healey Sprite

LOW built to corner with minimum roll, the Sprite combines protection for the driver with good all-round vision.

Motoring That is Fun at Very Modest Cost

WERE it possible to define quantitatively a pleasure-to-price ratio for cars, the new Austin-Healey Sprite would undoubtedly register an amazingly high figure for this desirable virtue. Costing about as much to buy as do many popular saloons of similar 1-litre engine size, and perhaps even cheaper than such saloons to run, this open two-seater offers much better acceleration up to a top speed which is higher by some 10 m.p.h., but responsiveness to the slightest touch on the controls is what really makes it such a joy to drive.

Small in size, the Sprite is certainly not a "miniature" car nor should it be regarded as merely a fragile toy. Modern full-width styling of the low-drag body enables it to provide generous room for two big men on excellent seats and there is substantial (if awkwardly arranged) accommodation for luggage also. Almost entirely in evenings and at week-ends,

and unable to attend motor races or other public functions in a still-secret car, members of our staff nevertheless ran the Sprite some 2,000 miles in a period of 20 days, at the end of which period a car which came to us with just over 2,000 miles on its speedometer merely seemed rather better for this extra running-in mileage.

Weighing 2-3-cwt. less than the saloons which use a basically similar power unit, and with wind resistance minimized by a 10-15-inch saving in overall height, the Sprite has required only mild engine tuning to gain performance fully comparable with lively modern saloons of double its size. There are two carburetters, and some valuable mechanical refinements inside the engine to ensure its stamina, but it retains a compression ratio which is moderate enough to tolerate the use of intermediate-grade fuels, a cast iron exhaust manifold with central hot-spot, and a camshaft giving touring valve timing. It is a docile engine, starting easily and quite happy to pull down to 15 m.p.h. in top gear if the car must be lent to some driver of non-sporting tastes. But it is an engine which only begins to sound alive in top gear at more than 30 m.p.h. and thereafter remains smooth and hard-working until the rev. counter needle reaches the far end of the scale, use of 5,000 r.p.m. in the gears when accelerating seeming entirely natural, and cautionary markings on the rev. counter dial between 5,500 and 6,000 r.p.m. being quickly reached. The exhaust note is sharp at wide throttle openings and high r.p.m., but with reasonably restrained handling the Sprite runs through towns without much noise.

Oil consumption during our test was only about 1 pint per 1,000 miles, but in exceptionally warm spring weather the coolant temperature rose sharply enough in London traffic or around Devon trials hills to suggest the desirability of some air outlet louvres on top of the bonnet.

Contributing much to the merit of this car is a four-speed synchromesh gearbox, third gear being useful up to an over-60 m.p.h. speed which is in sensible relation to an over-80 m.p.h. maximum in top gear. The gap between 3rd and 2nd ratios is too wide to please really hard drivers, the useful limit of speed in 2nd gear being less than 40 m.p.h., but this ratio will, if required, start the car from rest and carries it up almost any hill which is used by normal traffic. Located with its knob rather high up and close to the facia, the remote-control gear lever is positive in action, but became stiff to use when the car was really well warmed up.

Rack and pinion steering is geared at only 2¼ turns from extremity to extremity of a steering lock which lets the car swing round between low kerbs a mere 30 feet apart. With no evident lost motion whatever, seemingly negligible friction, and quite light self-centring effect, this steering lets the car be guided by use of fingers and wrists rather than by arm movements —the near-vertical two-spoke wheel is set too close to the seat to permit the straight-arm driving position which is fashionable with racing drivers of cars with lower-geared steering. Naturally enough, this is a car which corners fast with little or no roll, squealing its tyres only under very severe provocation, and in a corner it shows a modest degree of

In Brief

Price £455 plus purchase tax £223 17s. 0d. equals £678 17s. 0d.

Capacity	948 c.c.
Unladen kerb weight	12¾ cwt.
Acceleration :	
20-40 m.p.h. in top gear	12.6 sec.
0-50 m.p.h. through gears	13.7 sec.
Maximum direct top gear gradient	1 in 11.7
Maximum speed	82.9 m.p.h.
"Maximile" speed	81.1 m.p.h.
Touring fuel consumption	43 m.p.g.
Gearing : 15.4 m.p.h. in top gear at 1,000 r.p.m. 30.8 m.p.h. at 1,000 ft./min. piston speed.	

The Austin-Healey Sprite

COCKPIT of this simple sports car shows the central gear lever and handbrake, individual bucket seats, two-spoke steering wheel, optional rev. counter and neatly fitted rubber floor covering.

pressures. Ordinary buyers of this car should never have any worry with brake fade, but the harder treatment imposed by competitions might disclose that whilst a single stop from 80 m.p.h. merely produces a warm smell, three or four stops from 60 m.p.h. in rapid succession cause a considerable temporary loss of front brake effectiveness. Set close against the passenger seat, the pull-up handbrake (of touring rather than fly-off pattern) works excellently. Low build and proximity of the radiator air intake to the ground limit this car's ability to negotiate fords or flood-water, but ground clearance beneath the chassis proves to be rather more adequate than it appears, as the underside of the body is a smooth metal surface almost devoid of vulnerable projections.

stable "understeer" until the limit of tyre adhesion is transgressed. Perhaps because the natural sensitivity of the steering is magnified by flexible rubber bushes in some of the front and rear suspension pivots, the car needs a decidedly delicate touch on the controls to put it into a corner fast and accurately on a chosen line without initial "oversteering" by the driver, and too heavy a hand on the controls will accentuate a slight tendency to weave on the straight at maximum speeds. Once a sensitive driver has the feel of this car however, he can revel in hustling it along winding roads, totally forgetting a tendency for the car to pull slightly to the right during acceleration or left on the over-run which

at first acquaintance was fairly evident. Wet and slippery roads do nothing to diminish the pleasure of driving this light and outstandingly responsive car, and rough roads do not jolt it unduly despite the suspension being much firmer than on most modern touring cars.

Toe and Heel

Three pedals which are spaced to accommodate reasonably wide shoes are set conveniently level with one another, and the headlamp dipper acts as a rest for the left foot beside the clutch pedal. It is possible to "blip" the accelerator for a downward gearchange whilst braking, and the brakes give instant and powerful response to modest pedal

Habitability

In respect of touring car amenities a sensible compromise seems to have been struck, the Sprite having most of the essentials included in its moderate price but being very evidently capable of improvement by the subsequent addition of extra equipment. Two front-hinged doors (with interior handles only) give acceptable ease of entry to the low body, and capacious pockets in the lower halves of unlined doors leave generous elbow width available above them. Two sidescreens have simple and secure fixings, and the fully detachable hood has a three-piece rear window of wrap-around proportions. Two wiper blades operate on a curved glass windscreen of large area, which gives good protection although inducing appreciable backdraught in the cockpit. Flashing turn indicators do not cancel themselves but their control is conveniently placed at the centre of the facia panel. An excellent driving light is given by the headlamps, though in misty weather the fact that their mountings are almost in the driver's short-range sight line over the low bonnet might prove a handicap. Unluckily, the pattern of air flow around the body at speeds above 60 m.p.h. tends to flutter the hood, and blows rainwater or insects into the body through gaps which open up between an easy-to-erect hood and the top of the windscreen, and between the windscreen and sidescreens. An optional extra, the fresh-air heater with air valve and booster fan controlled from the facia panel worked well on our test car, and by turning off the under-bonnet water tap it could be used to blow cool air into the cockpit. Accommodation for a considerable volume of luggage is available behind the seats, in a long and reasonably wide compartment of moderate height, but this space can be reached only from the front

BENEATH the lift-up body nose is this 948 c.c. engine, with twin carburetters and modified internally to withstand sustained operation at high r.p.m.

(Continued on page 603)

B20

The Austin-Healey Sprite

past tilted-forward seat backrests, and small items can become lost in its depths. The hood fabric and sidescreens must be stowed in the luggage space when they are not in use, the folded hood frame fitting neatly into sockets where it encircles the mouth of the luggage compartment, but contributing to the variety of minor rattles evident around

TAILPIECE of the small Austin-Healey is a luggage locker accessible only from inside the body. Weather protection includes a quickly erected hood with wrap-around rear window.

what is in essentials a sturdily rigid body.

Simple in its mechanical design, and using a large proportion of well-tried components this should not be in any way a difficult car to maintain. Proper provision is made, for example, for access to the gearbox dipstick, a secure cover being disclosed when the moulded rubber floor covering is rolled back. Concealed hinges do not allow the awkwardly heavy lift-up nose of the steel body to rise as far as is desirable for comfortable access to the engine, but two self-locking struts can be supplemented by a third prop to ensure the safety of anyone working on the mechanism. Even when driven quite hard this car gives over 30 m.p.g. fuel economy, and gentler treatment readily produces well over 40 m.p.g. on long runs when the petrol tank capacity of 6 gallons begins to seem less meagre.

It is safe to predict that this inexpensive new Austin-Healey will have a very wide appeal, both in Britain and in many other parts of the world. Good performance which asks to be used to the full, controls of a responsiveness which many touring car owners have never even imagined possible, and a complete lack of temperament will make it a desirable and possible purchase both as an " only " car and also as " second car " in households already using a four-seat saloon.

A full description of the Sprite appears on pages 622-625.

Specification

Engine:

Cylinders	4
Bore	62.9 mm.
Stroke	76.2 mm.
Cubic capacity	948 c.c.
Piston area	19.29 sq. in.
Valves	Pushrod o.h.v.
Compression ratio	8.3/1
Carburetter	2 inclined S.U. type H1
Fuel pump	AC mechanical
Ignition timing control	Centrifugal and vacuum
Oil filter	Tecalemit or Purolator, full-flow
Max. power (net)	43 b.h.p. (gross, 50 b.h.p.)
at	5,200 r.p.m.
Piston speed at max. b.h.p.	2,600 ft./min.

Transmission

Clutch	Borg and Beck 6¼-in. s.d.p.
Top gear (s/m)	4.22
3rd gear (s/m)	5.96
2nd gear (s/m)	10.02
1st gear	15.31
Reverse	19.69
Propeller shaft	Hardy Spicer open
Final drive	Hypoid bevel
Top gear m.p.h. at 1,000 r.p.m.	15.4
Top gear m.p.h. at 1,000 ft./min. piston speed	30.8

Chassis

Brakes	Lockheed hydraulic (2 l.s. front)
Brake drum internal diameter	7 in.
Friction lining area	67.5 sq. in.
Suspension:	
Front	Independent by coil springs and wishbones
Rear	Quarter elliptic springs and rigid axle
Shock absorbers	Armstrong hydraulic, lever-arm type
Steering gear	Rack and pinion
Tyres	5.20-13 tubeless

Coachwork and Equipment

Starting handle .. .. Yes
Battery mounting .. Behind engine on scuttle
Jack Bipod screw type with ratchet handle
Jacking points External sockets on body sides
Standard tool kit: Jack and ratchet handle, tyre pump, grease gun, wheel nut spanner, ignition screwdriver/feeler, tyre valve key, sparking plug spanner, plug and tappet feeler gauge, screwdriver, toolbag.
Exterior lights: 2 headlamps, 2 sidelamps/flashers, 2 stop/tail lamps, number plate lamp.
Number of electrical fuses: 2
Direction indicators: Flashers (white front, amber rear), non self-cancelling.
Windscreen wipers: 2-blade electrical, self-parking.
Windscreen washers: Optional extra.
Sun vizors: None
Instruments: Speedometer with decimal trip distance recorder, oil pressure gauge, coolant thermometer, fuel contents gauge (tachometer optional extra).
Warning lights: Headlamp main beam, direction indicators, dynamo charge.
Locks: With ignition key: Ignition switch. With other keys: None
Glove lockers: None
Map pockets: Two in doors
Parcel shelves: None
Ashtrays: None
Cigar lighters: None
Interior lights: Instrument lighting only
Interior heater: Optional extra, fresh-air type with screen de-misters.
Car radio: Optional extra
Extras available: Rev. Counter, Heater, Radio, Screen washers, laminated glass screen, front bumper, tonneau cover, locking petrol cap.
Upholstery material: Leathercloth
Floor covering: Moulded rubber mats
Exterior colours standardized. Five
Alternative body styles: None

Maintenance

Sump 6 pints, plus ⅞ pint in filter, S.A.E. 30 (below freezing, S.A.E. 20W)
Gearbox .. .. .. 2½ pints, S.A.E. 30
Rear axle 1¾ pints, S.A.E. 90 hypoid gear oil
Steering gear lubricant S.A.E. 90 hypoid gear oil
Cooling system capacity 5¾ pints (2 drain taps)
Chassis lubrication: By oil gun every 1,000 miles to 10 points
Ignition timing .. .. 5° before t.d.c. static
Contact breaker-gap .. 0.014–0.016 in.
Sparking plug type Champion N5 (14 mm. long reach)
Sparking plug gap .. .. 0.025 in.
Valve timing Inlet opens 5° before t.d.c. and closes 45° after b.d.c.: Exhaust opens 40° before b.d.c. and closes 10° after t.d.c.
Tappet clearances (Hot) Inlet and exhaust 0.012 in.
Front wheel toe-in .. .. 0 – 1/8 in.
Camber angle .. .. 1°
Castor angle .. .. 3°
Steering swivel pin inclination .. 6½°
Tyre pressures:
Front .. .. 18 lb.
Rear .. .. 20 lb.
Brake fluid .. .. .. Lockheed
Battery type and capacity: 12 volt, 43 amp. hr. Lucas B.T.W.7A.

823

The Motor   422   *April 22, 1959*

90-PLUS SPRITE

A Warwick-tuned Austin-Healey

Hardtop, disc brakes, wire wheels and dual exhaust system make the car about half a hundredweight heavier, even though the front bumper is removed.

ROADWORTHINESS, an engine which is already lively and has proved its ability to withstand the stress of developing much more power, even the name Austin-Healey Sprite itself, have been an open invitation from the start to specialist tuners of production cars. From the Healey works in Warwick there came into our hands recently a Sprite which has "got about as far as they can go," possessing not only a considerably modified engine but altered transmission ratios and several changes in the chassis specification, of which the most notable are centre-lock wire wheels and disc front brakes.

The result is a machine lifted out of the amusing runabout class into the ranks of serious sports cars, breaking from modern tradition in providing high performance with a fair amount of noise and fuss (but complete reliability) from a very small engine.

It is unfortunate that an aggressive and tiring bark from the exhaust, resonating at between about 2,300 r.p.m. and 3,000 r.p.m., is the most immediately noticeable characteristic of the car, the more so as the noisy speeds are not those corresponding with the greatest increase in performance. The biggest gains are to be found, as might be expected, at the upper end of the scale, where better breathing of the engine is exploited to achieve a mean maximum speed of 91.6 m.p.h., equal to just under 6,500 r.p.m.

A table on this page shows the cost of the several items and operations applied to the test car. So far as the engine is concerned they mainly represent "Tuning Condition 4" in the Sprite Tuning Booklet, a condition which apart from the aforementioned exhaust note leaves the engine flexible, easy to start from hot or cold and perfectly docile, although a diet of 100-octane fuel becomes imperative. One serious drawback for touring use is the omission of the fan, without which the radiator soon boils in standstill traffic jams. Trumpet-shaped inlet pipes replace the air-cleaners and separate tail pipes take exhaust gases from the middle and outer pairs of cylinders. The test car was fitted with 1¼-in. S.U. carburetters in place of the normal 1⅛-in. components. This modification, which is probably more useful at high than at low speeds, is unfortunately no longer available.

The 4.55 : 1 rear axle ratio is lower than standard. A close-ratio gearbox giving overall ratios in the indirect gears of 6.14, 9.05 and 13.67 : 1 which was also fitted on the car supplied for test has been discontinued. Normal indirect ratios with the 4.55 : 1 axle would be 5.53, 9.30 and 14.21 : 1.

Fast and accelerative in a straight line, the modified Sprite is also an extremely roadworthy sports car. Without sacrifice of the quick steering which is one of the normal Sprite's

PERFORMANCE

(See text for note on parts no longer available)

	Normal Sprite (The Motor Road Test, May 21, 1958)	Modified Sprite
Instruments		
Speedometer at 30 m.p.h.	3% fast	12% fast
Speedometer at 60 m.p.h.	5% fast	13% fast
Distance recorder	2% fast	7% fast
Acceleration in top gear		
10–30 m.p.h.	13.7 sec.	12.2 sec.
20–40 m.p.h.	12.6 sec.	10.4 sec.
30–50 m.p.h.	12.6 sec.	11.7 sec.
40–60 m.p.h.	14.4 sec.	13.9 sec.
50–70 m.p.h.	18.5 sec.	13.2 sec.
60–80 m.p.h.	—	19.1 sec.
Acceleration from standstill[*]		
0–30 m.p.h.	5.1 sec.	5.0 sec.
0–50 m.p.h.	13.7 sec.	11.6 sec.
0–70 m.p.h.	31.1 sec.	24.0 sec.
Standing quarter-mile	21.8 sec.	20.7 sec.
Maximum speed	82.9 m.p.h.	91.6 m.p.h.
Fuel consumption		
At constant 30 m.p.h.	52.5 m.p.g.	47.0 m.p.g.
At constant 50 m.p.h.	53.5 m.p.g.	45.5 m.p.g.
At constant 70 m.p.h.	36.0 m.p.g.	37.5 m.p.g.
Overall fuel consumption	33.6 m.p.g.	30.5 m.p.g.

Brakes from 30 m.p.h.

Normal	Modified
0.97g with 90 lb. pressure.	1.0g with 140 lb. pressure.
0.75g with 75 lb. pressure.	0.96g with 96 lb. pressure.
0.49g with 50 lb. pressure.	0.67g with 75 lb. pressure.
0.22g with 25 lb. pressure.	0.47g with 50 lb. pressure.
	0.30g with 25 lb. pressure.

*Using close-ratio gearbox no longer available.

pleasantest features, the fitting of a front anti-roll bar and possibly the wider track resulting from knock-off Rudge hubs have produced a more stable car with slight but consistent understeer. The modifications include stronger valves on both front and rear dampers, improving the already excellent road-holding at some cost in riding comfort.

With the extra weight of wire wheels, disc front brakes, larger rear drums and a shapely reinforced plastic hard-top, but lightened of its front bumper, the car weighed-in unladen at about ½ cwt. heavier than its normal counterpart, a weight which the new brakes cope with most easily and reassuringly; stopping is stable even from high speed on a wet road. As an alternative and less costly conversion it is possible to have wire wheels with the existing drum brakes.

All the modifications listed here are carried out after purchase, in order to avoid a heavy increase in purchase tax which would be payable if the costs were included in the price of a complete new car. For the complete set of extras (excluding those which do not relate directly to performance or road-worthiness) the total to be added to the Sprite's £631 11s. British price is just over £166. plus charges for fitting.

CONVERSION BY ITEMS

		£	s.	d.
Engine				
Pistons for 9.3:1 compression ratio		9	10	0
Camshaft		6	0	0
Distributor		5	10	0
Valve springs			15	4
1¼-in. carburetters	no longer available			
Modifying and polishing cylinder head		10	0	0
Dual exhaust system		11	0	0
Transmission				
Close-ratio gearbox	no longer available			
4.55:1 rear axle		23	0	0
Chassis				
Wire wheel and disc brake set		89	0	0
Stronger front and rear damper valves		3	0	0
Front anti-roll bar		8	10	0
Body				
Hardtop with sliding windows		46	10	0
Quick action filler cap		2	4	0

Rudge hubs make the front and rear tracks noticeably wider without altering the suspension, to which a front anti-roll bar is added. Girling disc front brakes are matched by larger drums on the rear wheels.

C16

As well as driving numerous borrowed versions, the author has run two red Sprites, the first one, MCF 149, here seen at a Silverstone club meeting, being modified for racing. The present car, YOL 267, has merely been personalized for comfortable everyday road work.

MOTORING FOR FUN

CASE HISTORY
OF A SPRITE

By J. W. Anstice Brown

The Small, Practical Austin-Healey, Used for Business and Pleasure, Provides Fun with Economy and Few Disadvantages

BEING a simple optimist by nature it has always been a source of wonder to me that it is only trouble that is reputed to come "in battalions." My feelings on this subject have been given substance of late by the number of examples of The British Motor Corporation's smallest sports car that seem to have positively overwhelmed me. I have raced Sprites, road-tested standard Sprites, tuned Sprites, used a Sprite as transport and yet perhaps the greatest compliment that can be paid to them all is that having owned one more or less from the day on which they were announced I still find no regret in stepping out of a very large majority of the road-test cars that it is my lot to drive and insinuating my six-foot-two back into my current version of this little car which, even in this present age. manages to possess that fast-vanishing asset. character.

Ownership of one of these cars started for me when I asked Marcus Chambers of the B.M.C. competitions department one Friday what the chances were of a Sprite on the following Monday so that I could enter it in an Irish road race to be held in three weeks time. They were, he assured me, quite definitely nil. but miracles do happen and once again the optimist was in luck and a car was ready for collection not on the Monday I had requested but on the one after that. leaving very little time for preparation before we set sail for the Emerald Isle. With help from many friends. Speedwell modifications were hastily added. the headlights brutally chiseled off. tubes put into the tyres, and harder Mintex brake linings fitted, all in the space of four days during which the hours of 9 to 5 were booked by less agreeable activities than fiddling with sports cars. Much to the amazement of one and all the race provided the first win for a Sprite.

More important. however. is the fact that the car was used for 8,000 miles during which it competed in sprints and races, and served as normal transport without even a decoke. With the exception of three coils which it devoured most avidly, nothing required replacement, and when it was sold, so far as I could tell, only new tyres were needed.

The realization that I should have to spend another £200 on the car to make it compete on level terms with those which were then appearing in the hands of other competitors. on top of the £800 that I reckoned the car had already cost in modified

form. decided me to part with it and race something which required less in the way of modification. and this I did. However. the necessity of a car in my present occupation presented the opportunity of running another Sprite. merely as bread and butter transport, but naturally deriving what pleasure I could from the fact that it was a sports car and also suffering any attendant disadvantages of running an open two-seater all the year round.

After a very much longer wait than was required for the first car, the second one arrived and was almost identical to the first, before it had been turned into a racer. Minor and much appreciated modifications were the repositioning of the coil and a new method of hood fastening at the front which, unlike the system employed on the previous car, actually does keep out rain and flies. the weather protection now being as good as could be desired. Apart from this and the registration number. however. it might be the same car. a fair indication that not much development of the design has proved necessary once it reached the production stage. The colour is red with red interior, as before.

This machine has now covered nearly 17.000 miles, shows very little signs of wear, and. as previously stated, there is still pleasure in making a journey in it. However. there is no clearer example of the inability to please all of the people all of the time than the motorcar and although I feel that the advantages of running a sports car on the road outweigh the disadvantages. it must be admitted that the disadvantages are there. The principal one is getting into the driving compartment. which makes the Sprite a car in which I would rather travel 50 miles than go shopping. entry and exit being difficult, although once inside there is a surprising amount of room. Equally. carrying oddments is not made simple by the lack of an outside opening for the boot. However. it must be said that, carefully packed. a vast amount of luggage can be carried and it is possible to carry three people in the car, with the hood up, over considerable distances in a reasonably comfortable manner.

Quarter elliptic rear springs (the front suspension is A35) definitely have advantages for the man who motors briskly as

c7

CASE HISTORY OF A SPRITE

The hood is now completely watertight, unlike the one on the earlier car. The original number plate which made lifting the heavy bonnet even more difficult has been replaced by the stick-on variety which fits between the headlamps which are powerful enough to allow full performance to be used at night.

The name on the back is all that gives a clue to the casual observer of the car's identity, so effective is the disguise provided by the Ashley Laminates hardtop. It is held in place by four small bolts and can be removed in well under ten minutes when the occasion demands.

of some sort is obtainable at any hour of the day or night, the range of stations being wide. This particular set is remarkably free from interference, the M1 bridges being one of the few things that affect its performance.

Whilst on the subject of extras, a few words about those fitted to the car may be of interest. A car, as well as being a means of transport, is also something personal and as such a certain type of motorist, amongst which I must include myself, revolts against owning just another mass-produced car similar in most respects to his neighbours. Unlike that protagonist of the performance-modified car for road use, Mr. Pomeroy, I go to the other extreme, believing that it is better to keep the mechanism as standard as possible and to use what is there fully for a longer time and as a result I am averse to any engine alterations which must accelerate wear and slightly affect reliability in the long run. Therefore, the only changes around the engine department are the fitting of platinum-pointed plugs in place of the normal ones which were reducing performance after 10,000 miles (the platinium ones are as new after 6,000-odd miles) and the replacement of the heater tap by a water valve controlled from the driving compartment, thus enabling either

(Continued on page 231)

anyone who has experienced axle tramp on a Morris Minor and then sampled a Sprite will testify. The suspension is, however, firm in the interests of handling, and a passenger not used to sports cars pronounced it one of the most uncomfortable rides he had ever experienced, but this is. of course, purely a matter of personal opinion as I myself far prefer this firmness to the soggy seasick-making feel of a softly sprung saloon. Less endearing is the tendency of the rear suspension to bottom on certain uneven road surfaces and the work that has been imposed upon it has produced the car's only real failure in that the offside front and rear road springs require replacing after 14,000 miles. It must, however, be admitted that little consideration has been shown to it when rough surfaces were encountered on the road. Curiously, however, the previous car, which was frequently overloaded with excess passengers and suffered the rigours of racing, showed no sign of developing this trouble.

The really noisy sports car is great fun on a short journey but for everyday use quietness is desirable for many reasons. The exhaust note of the Sprite is little different from that of a saloon and the engine is turbine-like in its smoothness and lack of mechanical clatter. The car is, in fact, only noisier than a saloon in respect of a few rattles emanating from the back (tool kit, spare wheel, etc., which could easily be eliminated should an owner so desire) and in the matter of wind roar, although this is less great when the hardtop is in place and could no doubt be reduced still further by the addition of sliding sidescreens (these have, incidentally, recently been standardized to replace the one-piece type on production Sprites). Although this noise is sufficient to make conversation tiring on a long run at speed, a Pye TCR2000 push-button wireless has been fitted and is found to work admirably, it even being possible to listen to plays when driving fast whilst music
c8

Under-bonnet changes from standard are few, consisting of platinum pointed plugs and a water valve for the heater fitted at the rear of the cylinder head. There is a tendency to bang one's head on the bonnet when working on the engine and the battery is not easy to service, but otherwise accessibility is good.

CASE HISTORY OF A SPRITE

Without exception the author has never found a car with a better-planned interior. The pedals allow heel and toe retardation, there is a resting place for the clutch foot, the steering wheel is well placed and all the dashboard controls fall readily to hand. Extras are the heater and water valve, wireless, rev. counter, hidden interior light and the invaluable windscreen-washer.

(Continued from Page 230)

hot or cold air to be obtained from the heater (which operates excellently but does fill the car with fumes in traffic) without stopping and delving under the bonnet. A rev. counter (an optional extra) and an interior light have been added. The latter is easily fitted under the rail at the top of the dashboard and is a very useful minor improvement which could, one feels, easily be incorporated at the factory. The major alteration, a recent one, is the fitting of a removable hardtop which was announced at the Racing Car Show by Ashley Laminates, specialists in glass fibre bodywork who, as well as producing their own shells, make bodies for Team Lotus. It is no small praise to say that one of the principal advantages of the hardtop is in the change which it effects in the appearance of the Sprite: this is so much so from the back that, when the car is parked, people have walked round to the front to discover what make it is. Draught reduction is a practical asset as is the parcel shelf by the rear window, although if it were covered in non-slip material of some sort it would be even more useful. Rear vision by way of the rear view mirror is vastly improved, but this is paid for by side blind spots which can be a nuisance at road junctions.

Lack of front bumpers and the use of stick-on front numbers further distinguish the car and complete the few alterations from standard; the only other addition that would, I feel, be worth while is a radiator blind (Sprites are, for some reason, very slow to warm up) and, were I a smoker, an ashtray, very necessary in a car where you cannot open the windows.

The road behaviour of the Sprite has been fully covered in *The Motor* road test, which appeared when it was announced, so most of its road characteristics should be well known, and the following details do not cover all facets of performance. Starting from cold the choke, which cannot be locked in

position, must be used for a considerable distance and performance is not good till the engine is warm. Thereafter the little engine is most willing and is not worried by high r.p.m., developing its power fairly high up the rev. range and feeling happier than when being slogged. The gearchange has been criticized in some quarters as being stiff to operate, but I have always found it extremely light and pleasant to use, this being true of all examples that I have driven. From approximately 60 m.p.h. on the overrun a strange transmission noise is evident but the previous car also made this sound and it has produced no ill effects so I have grown used to it, as one does for instance, to the jingle of the starting handle of one of the car's distant predecessors—the Austin Ruby.

Roadholding is of a very high order, although the vehicle, being very light and having sensitive steering, can reach the point of no return rather quickly if severely provoked. Oversteer is prominent and when cornering quickly the technique is to unwind the lock a fraction before the corner really ends and this will produce a smooth change of direction. In the wet the roadholding is quite exceptional although my previous car was somewhat better than the present one, due, I suspect, to the fact that its wheels had been balanced. Recommended pressure for the tyres is 18 p.s.i., but I find that 24 p.s.i. front and 26 p.s.i. rear suits me better and complete lack of tyre squeal at these pressures is a frequent point of complimentary comment from passengers.

On borrowing the car for a day or two, a member of *The Motor* staff remarked that if he drove it to work every day in place of his six-seater saloon he would arrive in a far better temper each morning, and this nippiness is one of the great advantages of owning this type of car. Light weight and a reasonable amount of power make it easy to gain that vital first few yards in the traffic-lights Grand Prix and the small overall size of the car makes it possible to wriggle into gaps where limousines fear to tread. This, and appearance, can, however, annoy the frustrated saloon-car driver and it is not possible to get away with some of the cheeky manœuvres which would pass unnoticed in a more ordinary machine without provoking angry hooting. A psychiatrist could no doubt tell me why.   *(Continued overleaf)*

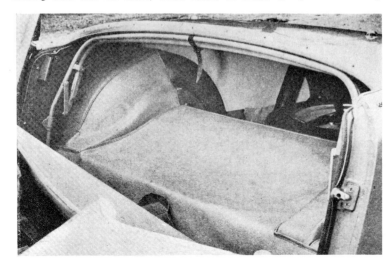

There is plenty of boot space although it is not as accessible as might be, and the position of the spare wheel, just visible, means that it must be kept reasonably clean.

CASE HISTORY OF A SPRITE

Six foot two of author emphasize the low build of the Sprite even when the roofline is raised by the hardtop. Once inside, there is plenty of room.

The Sprite being higher geared than the A35, for instance, which uses the same engine, nippiness around town is not coupled with fussiness on the open road and even the length of the Motorway is quite bearable at a cruising speed around a genuine 70 m.p.h. whilst on main roads it is possible to average 55 m.p.h. when traffic density is low.

There is little sign of wear anywhere, a passenger recently remarking that the Sprite still had the taut feel of a new car. A pint of oil is usually required every 2,000 miles, just as a change is due anyway, the car actually seeming to have a greater appetite for water, another somewhat inexplicable Sprite characteristic. Petrol is consumed at the very reasonable rate of 35.9 m.p.g., although this has shown a tendency to rise slightly of late and checks with a compression tester indicate that a decoke would not be out of place, which probably accounts for the increased thirst. The tubeless tyres have behaved well and will, I feel, last until over 20,000 miles are completed without incorporating the spare which is stored in such a manner that it is desirable to keep it clean and therefore not use it if possible. Thereafter a set of Michelin " X " will be fitted in order to gain experience of how these somewhat controversial tyres behave over a considerable mileage. Brake linings are wearing and will require replacement ere long but otherwise I do not envisage any major replacements. The dust from the linings, incidentally, cannot escape, and it pays to remove the drums and blow this out every 5,000 miles.

Minor ills have been a shattered windscreen, replaced by a laminated one which promptly cracked, a burst water hose, failure of both stoplights and one slow puncture. Starting with very little chrome there is not much to go rusty and the paintwork has stood up to City use very well, only a few chips having been knocked off the bumperless (another extra) front by flying stones. The driver's seat shows slight signs of use whilst the passenger's is as new. The floor mats, which never fitted anyway, are tearing and are one of the few parts which do not do the rest of the car credit.

A point which struck me when a colleague recently tested his everyday transport and reported on it was the discrepancy between the top end figures which he obtained and those of a similar model we had recently road-tested, and it is interesting to note a similar drop in performance in the Sprite figures. In this case the widely varying weather conditions and the different test venues account for some of the differences and the need for decarbonization also has effect. As a matter of interest it is, however, my intention to discover how much must be done to bring the car back to full performance and report thereon. The increase in speed when the hard top is in position is commendable.

Here, then, is a car which has provided me with thoroughly efficient and reliable transport and, at the cost of a few, in my opinion, quite minor disadvantages of the type associated with the refined modern sports car, far more fun and far less frustration than I could ever have obtained from a saloon.

c12

AUSTIN-HEALEY SPRITE COMPARATIVE TESTS

"The Motor" Road Test, 1958	1959 Sprite after approx. 17,000 miles
Weather	
Warm and dry with moderate breeze. (Temperature 70°—74°F.; Barometer 30.2—30.4 in. Hg.)	Wet with 10 to 34 m.p.h. wind. (Temperature 42°—44°F.; Barometer 29.4—29.2 in. Hg.)
Kerb Weight	
12¾ cwt.	13¾ cwt.

Maximum Speeds

Mean of 4 opposite ¼-mile runs:		Mean lap of banked track:	
Open	—	Open	73.1 m.p.h.
Hood erect	82.9 m.p.h.	Hood erect	77.3 m.p.h.
Hardtop	—	Hardtop	79.1 m.p.h.
Best ¼ mile:		Best ¼ mile:	
Open	—	Open	76.3 m.p.h.
Hood erect	86.5 m.p.h.	Hood erect	79.6 m.p.h.
Hardtop	—	Hardtop	82.9 m.p.h.

Acceleration times on upper ratios

M.p.h.	top sec.	3rd sec.		top sec.	3rd sec.
10–30	13.7	8.6		13.5	8.4
20–40	12.6	7.7		12.1	7.5
30–50	12.6	8.6		13.7	8.6
40–60	14.4	11.4		19.2	—

Steady speed fuel consumption

	m.p.h.	m.p.g.	m.p.g.
At constant	30	52.5	46.5
At constant	40	54.5	45.4
At constant	50	53.5	41.0
At constant	60	38.0	40.0
At constant	70	36.0	32.6

Hill Climbing—at sustained steady speeds

Max. gradient on top gear—1 in 11.7 (Tapley 190 lb./ton)	1 in 12.7 (Tapley 176 lb./ton)
Max. gradient on 3rd gear—1 in 7.5 (Tapley 295 lb./ton)	1 in 8.4 (Tapley 264 lb./ton)
Max. gradient on 2nd gear—1 in 4.5 (Tapley 485 lb./ton)	1 in 5.1 (Tapley 429 lb./ton)

Instruments

Speedometer at 30 m.p.h.	3% fast	6.3% fast
Speedometer at 60 m.p.h.	5% fast	7.3% fast
Distance recorder	2% fast	2.5% fast

Compression Pressures
(On 1959 Sprite only)
Cyls. 1 to 4 respectively—
At 1,200 miles: 150; 153; 148; 140. (lb./sq. in.)
At 16,750 miles: 127; 125; 122; 120. (lb./sq. in.)

THE AUTOCAR, 25 AUGUST 1961

IMPROVING THE PERFORMANCE OF POPULAR CARS

Above: The car which was tested competes at an International Silverstone meeting with Australian, Paul Hawkins, at the wheel. Below: Not after the fire . . . but it shows the lengths to which competitors go to remove all surplus weight

SEBRING SPRITE

ALTHOUGH many different conversions of standard production cars come the way of *The Autocar* Road Test staff, few have been so internationally famous in competition motoring as the Austin-Healey Sebring Sprite. This car, perhaps, only just falls within the category of a conversion, since the modifications are extensive enough for it to be regarded as a separate model. Although based on the normal Sprite, it has been built in sufficient numbers for the car to be recognized and homologated as a Grand Tourer by the international authorities.

It is available in a number of different forms, depending on the uses to which the owner wishes to put it. The actual car tested belonged to John Sprinzel and has covered many hundreds of racing miles—some of them with Stirling Moss at the wheel.

Few distinguishable Sprite features remained. The B.M.C. A-type engine had been modified extensively—a formula Junior crankshaft, lightened flywheel, flat-top solid skirt pistons, over-size inlet valves and 11 to 1 compression ratio being among the changes. The fan had been removed, but a full-flow oil cooler helped to keep the temperature down. Mounted immediately behind the driving seat were two S.U. petrol pumps

PERFORMANCE

From rest through gears to:	Sebring Sprite	Mark 2 Sprite
40 m.p.h.	5·8 sec	9·0 sec
50 ,,	7·6 ,,	13·8 ,,
60 ,,	10·8 ,,	19·8 ,,
70 ,,	14·1 ,,	29·4 ,,
80 ,,	20·2 ,,	51·8 ,,
90 ,,	27·8 ,,	—
Standing quarter mile	17·8 sec	21·8 sec
Second Gear		
10—30 m.p.h.	5·6 sec	6·2 sec
20—40 ,,	4·0 ,,	6·1 ,,
30—50 ,,	4·3 ,,	—
Third Gear		
30—50 m.p.h.	5·7 sec	9·5 sec
40—60 ,,	5·7 ,,	11·3 ,,
50—70 ,,	6·5 ,,	—
Top Gear		
40—60 m.p.h.	8·6 sec	16·6 sec
50—70 ,,	9·5 ,,	19·2 ,,
70—90 ,,	14·2 ,,	—

Maximum Speed in Gears

Gear:			
Top (mean)	100 m.p.h. (7,200 r.p.m.)	85·3 m.p.h.
(best)	100 ,,	85·5 ,,
Third	73 ,,	68 ,,
Second	51 ,,	46 ,,
First	31 ,,	28 ,,

294

Modifications under the light-weight bonnet had been carried out in a workman-like style, and accessibility to all components is outstandingly good

SEBRING SPRITE . . .

for supplying the twin 1½in. S.U. carburettors; a nine-spring competition clutch transmitted the torque. A power output of 80 b.h.p. at 7,000 r.p.m. is claimed.

The gearbox was the close-ratio unit now fitted as standard equipment to the Mark II Sprite. Normally the Sebring Sprite has a 4·55:1 rear axle ratio, but on the car tested a 4·875:1 axle ratio was installed. This was the ratio employed at Brands Hatch, where the car had been racing a few days before it was collected for test. Suspension changes consisted of heavy-duty shock absorbers at the front with an anti-roll bar, and adjustable dampers at the rear. Wire wheels and 5·20—13in. R5 Dunlop covers were fitted. The front drum brakes had been replaced by 8·5in. diameter discs.

The bodywork had been extensively lightened; the bonnet was constructed from glass fibre and an aluminium hardtop of streamlined shape covered the passenger compartment. All the interior trim had been removed, and the battery shifted from under the bonnet to a position just forward of the rear axle. With the spare wheel on board and the 12-gallon fuel tank half-full, the car weighed 11·75 cwt, almost 2 cwt lighter than a standard hardtop Sprite. The weight distribution was almost exactly 50 per cent fore and aft.

First impression after opening the door, which was done by inserting a hand through a small sliding pane in the side-screen and lifting an interior catch, is one of bareness and exposed wiring. The whole of the facia had been removed and the only instruments fitted were an electronic tachometer, an oil pressure gauge, a water thermometer and a petrol gauge. Switches for lamps, ignition, starter and windscreen wiper were mounted on the central console which covered the gearbox and flywheel. Both the road and the rear axle are visible through gaps in the floor on either side of the battery box.

The first thing that one notices as soon as the engine starts, which it always did very easily, is the noise. Even the most hardened extrovert would be embarrassed by the amount of exhaust noise from this car. It is almost impossible to avoid it, however carefully one drives. In town the car was a slight nuisance, as it was inclined to overheat and even the soft plugs started to misfire. It also became very warm in the cockpit and one sat in a mist of Castrol-R fumes—very intoxicating for the diehard enthusiasts. Surprisingly enough, the engine was remarkably tractable, and one could potter along at relatively low engine speeds. Full power from the engine was not available under 5,000 r.p.m., but it then continued right through to 7,000 r.p.m. Rather fierce for road use, the clutch was much as one would have expected on a competition car.

On the open road, if one could submerge the feeling of being anti-social, the car was immense fun to drive. Hard when travelling slowly, the suspension and ride greatly improved with increased speed. The small bucket seats held their occupants

securely. Steering was light, direct and positive, the rack and pinion mechanism being very well run in. Gone was the "darting" feeling experienced with many Sprites and directional stability was excellent. While cornering the good balance of the car made the steering almost completely neutral and gave considerable confidence.

What of the performance? John Sprinzel had asked that the engine speed be limited to 7,200 r.p.m. In practice it was found that the engine started misfiring if this speed were exceeded. With the lower rear axle ratio incorporated it was possible to achieve 7,200 r.p.m. in top gear with remarkable ease, even up a slight incline. This engine speed represented about 100 m.p.h. Acceleration, therefore, not maximum speed, is the interesting feature of this car. In the performance table, the figures obtained are set out alongside those of the recently tested Mark II Sprite. A standing quarter-mile of 17·8sec is extremely fast, as is 0-80 m.p.h. in 20·2sec. In racing trim, with only one person aboard and no road test equipment, these figures naturally would be even better.

The disc brakes fitted on the front of the car are an obvious must for the Sebring Sprite. With these there was never any fade when stopping from high speeds frequently and consecutively.

Total price of the equipment fitted to this car is £650, and there is no reason why the modifications should not be made to a second-hand Sprite. In this case, for just over £1,000 one can have an extremely worth-while racing or rally car to distinguish itself in any international company. Its successes have been widespread and varied, and last year one finished third in the most gruelling of all rallies, the Liège-Rome-Liège, and its name results from regular class victories at Sebring.

The Mosses, brother and sister, sprint across the track to jump into their Sprites at the start of the Sebring four-hour Grand Touring car race earlier this year

Safety Harness Lesson

AT a recent Silverstone club race meeting there was a sharp reminder that safety harness is not an infallible saver. A two-door saloon, in which the squabs of the front seats fold forward to gain access to the rear, hit a bank head-on at moderate speed. The driver was wearing a full safety harness of a well-known and approved type. Force of impact, however, resulted in the seat coming off its mountings, and there appeared to be no locking device to stop the front seats jack-knifing in such a situation.

Under such conditions the full harness had little more effect than a lap strap, and the driver was badly cut about the face as a result of being thrown against the lower half of the steering wheel. It is suspected that the injury was aggravated because the harness was not done up sufficiently tightly.

There are three lessons to be learnt from this accident: A seat that hinges forward must be secured firmly at the rear; manufacturers should give careful attention to seat mountings; and a loosely worn harness is not properly effective.

OWNER'S VIEW

Lindsay R. Porter interviews Peter Baker, a thirty-nine year old Mk I Sprite enthusiast who lives in Worcestershire, England. Peter is a sales representative and is married, with two children.

L.R.P: I've often seen you pottering around in your 'Frogeye' on pleasant days this summer. How long have you been keen on the cars?

P.B. That's not really as straightforward a question as it might seem. This isn't my first 'Frog', you see. The first was bought by another 'me' in another phase of my life, before the kids and the mortgage and the grey hairs came along. It was a cherry red car and I remember seeing it parked in a garage forecourt in Worcester as I drove past, taking my wife to work — it must have been 1967; certainly before our eldest was born. After a few days of shooting glances at the car as I drove past in my old split-screen Minor, I finally plucked up courage and went in to take a look at it. I never really intended buying it at that point but before I knew it, I was signing on the bottom line of the Hire Purchase papers. He must have been a marvellous salesman — or perhaps it was just that I really wanted the car and didn't take much persuasion. I then had the problem of explaining it away to the wife ... but when she saw it — she'd never even noticed it driving past — she was over the moon!

L.R.P: How reliable was that first car?

P.B.: Bloody marvellous! I've never had one as good since! The water temperature gauge never worked at all and the cost of replacement nearly scared me to death, so I just left it and there were a couple of rattles that I never sorted out but it never gave a moment's trouble — oh, apart from once, when we were on holiday in the South of France. The fan belt went on the N86 and I didn't notice it in time to stop the engine boiling.

L.R.P: Most people would never have the nerve to go so far in a 'Frogeye'. Where on earth did you put all the luggage?

P.B.: You've obviously never tried putting luggage into a 'Frog'! Not only did we have ordinary luggage with us but we had a two-man tent as well. But that boot is really cavernous and you can get an enormous amount in. I remember, we put a rack on the back — I sent away for it specially for the trip. Got it from Pride & Clarke, or somewhere like that. In the end all we put on it was the spare wheel. The thing is, with the spare in its usual place and the boot full of luggage, you can't get at it if you have a puncture, short of laboriously taking every bit of your luggage out first. And in the case of a Sprite that's no easy matter. You need to be as agile as a contortionist and have arms like a monkey to squeeze everything into the big hole behind the front seats. Fortunately, we didn't have a puncture anyway. It would have been a problem because I left the jack in the boot!

L.R.P: How comfortable was your trip?

P.B.: Surprisingly good, actually. I found that I could really stretch my legs out and, being younger, didn't mind the noise and the hard suspension. As a matter of fact, I enjoyed zooming round those heavily cambered French minor roads with the top down. It was a great way of keeping cool and none of those little rear engined cars could get a look-in, though being French, they always try, don't they?

L.R.P: Did the car attract much attention in France?

P.B: Yes, people would just look at it with a big smile all over their faces as we drove past, especially in the towns. Coming back, by the way, we came a lot of the way with the top down. It was great for driving through the towns where you really have to be quite alert. The combination of responsive throttle and steering and all-round vision was really terrific!

L.R.P: You obviously had some really good times with that car. Why did you sell it?

P.B: I often wondered afterwards! But at the time we were buying our first house. We had just enough for the deposit but not enough for anything else. It was the middle of winter and it just seemed that a few sticks of furniture and some carpets were more important than the car at the time. In any case, we couldn't have kept it for very much longer because before long we started a family.

L.R.P: Was it simply nostalgia that led you to buy your present Mk I Sprite?

P.B. Yes, I'm sure that had a lot to do with it, but I really do admire that car for its virtues as well. I mean, it's quite amazing that such a cheap little car should have what was quite an adventurous rear suspension layout. A lot of people blame the rear suspension for giving the car twitchy handling, but I don't think it's as bad as most people make out. I always fitted the cheapest tyres I could get to my first car and they, of course, were crossply. I've got Michelin XZX on this one and I find that it has cut down on twitchiness to the point where I never notice it. Perhaps the old crossplies used to follow the undulations in the road surfaces.

L.R.P: What sort of condition was your present car in when you bought it?

P.B. I bought it from a chap in Merthyr, South Wales, through an advert. in *Exchange & Mart* about three years ago now. I looked at it fairly closely but obviously not closely enough. It failed its first MoT on a fair number of basic things such as corroded brake lines and badly worn front suspension – it really makes you wonder how it passed its previous test – but I didn't mind those things too much. When I found rust bubbling through around the rear wheel arches I took it in to my local body repairers and told them to hunt out any signs of rust they could find. I nearly died of shock when they told me what they had found. The inner sills were in a terrible state and so was much of the floor. Both rear wings needed quite a bit of work doing on them as well. I had all the work carried out on the basis that once it was done, it wouldn't need doing again as I really do look after the car. I get a Company car of course, because of my job, and so I suppose I find it easier than most to justify spending this sort of money on what is basically my hobby.

L.R.P: How often do you use your car?

P.B: I go to all the club meetings I can get to, whatever the weather, but otherwise I only use it at weekends when the weather is fine.

L.R.P: Has your car won any prizes in Concours or similar events?

P.B: I've never entered it in any such events. The car is mine and I don't need or want any one else to pass judgement on it. I enjoy looking at other people's 'Frogs' whether in the Concours or not and I enjoy talking to the owners and swapping tales of problems and a few tall stories!

L.R.P: Do you have any problems in obtaining parts for your car?

P.B: None whatever. I'm lucky I suppose because I live fairly close to Spridgebits who carry a lot of stock for Mk I Sprites, but I've used other specialists in the past when I've been near one when on the road. I suppose that the parts were used in so many other cars that they'll never run out.

L.R.P: Have you found it useful to belong to any particular one-make club?

P.B: When I first bought the car I made the mistake of joining the M.G. Owner's Club, thinking of the connection with Midgets. In fact, I first heard of Spridgebits through them but later I joined the Austin-Healey Owners' Club which is better suited to the needs of the 'Frog' owner. The M.G.O.C. seems a first class club, but it's better suited to the later cars, I think.

L.R.P: How would you sum up the enjoyment you get from your 'Frogeye' Sprite?

P.B: Quite simply, it's a young car in every sense of the word. It doesn't have any sophisticated gadgetry attached to it, so its appeal is plain and simple and that also makes it easy to maintain. It's young in appearance because it even *looks* like a happy, fun loving car and, best of all for me I suppose, it reminds me of when I was younger.

BUYING

Because only a tiny number of production changes were made to the Mk I Sprite during its production life, to all intents and purposes, there was only ever one 'Frogeye' produced, so the dilemma about which model of car to look for, which may afflict the potential owner of most other makes and models of car is avoided by the Sprite owner-to-be. Certainly, the early hood fixing system left something to be desired in that it introduced the owner to rather more of the elements than he or she might have bargained for and the early side-screens were less than totally practical in that it was impossible to open them, short of taking them right off. On the other hand, so few cars exist today with those original fittings in place that if the searcher should come across a car fitted with either or both of those items, he should congratulate himself on having made a find of almost archeological importance!

These areas apart, little choice exists except the condition, originality and price of the car. Striking a balance between these three is most important and it is also important that the prospective purchaser decides beforehand where his or her priorities lie. Unless money is no object, or unless an extraordinarily lucky find is made, a compromise will have to

be made. The choice for the enthusiast who is determined to have the most original and best condition car that can be obtained lies between paying a great deal for money for a concours or near concours car, or paying a great deal of money for having the car restored; indeed, the cost of restoration, bearing in mind today's high prices, frequently exceeds the highest value placed on a Sprite on the open market. One way around the problem for the potential owner with enough determination is d.i.y. With the aid of the excellent specialists who exist to serve the needs of Mk I and later Sprite owners, virtually every repair panel imaginable is obtainable – albeit at a price. The *Haynes MG Midget and A-H Sprite Owners Workshop Manual* is full of vital information for the home restorer and the Haynes/Foulis publication *MG Midget/A-H Sprite – A Guide to Purchase and DIY Restoration* contains all the information necessary to enable the enthusiast to carry out the work at home.

Many, if not most, Mk I Sprites are fitted with non-original parts. Some of these are highly undesirable and, in the case of a car that is supposed to be in first class condition should be looked at askance. Top of the list of price-reducing undesirability must be the fibreglass bonnet to which so many owners resorted in years gone by when these things mattered less. Other items to be avoided are the wrong wheels (although originals are fairly easily obtainable second hand), dashboard modifications, which are very common and not at all easy to put right, incorrect instruments and cars fitted with the wrong engine – check the engine number. Flared arches should be avoided like the plague because of the cost of restoring the bodywork to its former state and wide wheels can be a source of problems to suspension and wheel bearings which were not designed to take the excessive loads placed upon them. A commonly 'bodged'

modification carried out in earlier years was to cut away the rear cockpit to make access to the rear storage area easier. Again the cost of remedying such butchery would be high. Steering wheels have usually been changed for a later, totally unsuitable type and engines are often embellished with inappropriate engine tuning goodies, although these can usually be removed as easily as they were fitted.

Some period modifications would be highly desirable additions if a car should be found fitted with them. These are topped by the Coventry Climax engine fitted by the Jack Brabham tuning concern and which made the car's performance startling by any standards. They are, of course, extremely rare and the chances of finding one remote in the extreme. Still, it hurts no one to dream! There is more chance of finding a car fitted with one of the original Healey wire wheel and disc brake conversions and this, also, would be a worthwhile and interesting addition to the car (They can be distinguished from later, standard discs by make; Healey-supplied discs were Girling, BMC used Lockheed). As mentioned elsewhere, a range of modifications were offered by the Warwick concern and any of them would be pleasant to have. Many early cars were fitted with the (Farina) A40's 8 inch brake drums, brake back plates and shoes and if these are found fitted it may be considered appropriate to leave them in place – certainly they come from the right era. The gearbox, too, has often been replaced by a unit from one of the later cars. Correct gearboxes had a smooth external surface while later 'boxes with modified synchromesh and a longer life in general, had a ribbed surface.

Looking at things from the other end, there are certain items of original specification which are real plus points if found fitted to the car under inspection. These include rubber mats (now rare in the extreme and usually replaced by carpets), the correct steering wheel, the correct seats, the bonnet badge, and it would be very pleasant indeed to have one of the original valve radios fitted into the space where it belongs, on the passenger side of the dash. Under the bonnet, hallmarks of originality are the correct dynamo complete with a functioning tachometer drive, a pair of brass topped $1\frac{1}{8}$ inch carbs — they were frequently replaced by the later $1\frac{1}{2}$ inch SUs with plastic screws in the dash pot tops, and a pair of original pancake air filters. Increasingly, new replica parts are being made for these cars but there are some such as the rubber mats and the tachometer drive which will never be replicated because of the cost involved.

Once a decision has been made as to which condition category of car to look for, it is simply a matter of going out and buying the right car — except that, unfortunately, there is nothing simple about it! Patience and determination are the most useful virtues here because advertisements are notoriously inaccurate in what they describe and it may be necessary to search for a long time. In the case of the Sprite, whose mechanical components were widely used across a range of small cars, the bodywork is the area to which the greatest attention should be paid. Not only is some corrosion bound to be evident after the passing of thirty years, but it is also likely that there will have been repairs — sometimes layers of repairs — carried out on the car's most vulnerable parts. The first place to check is the area around the rear spring boxes. Look at the rear 'bulkhead' where the springs enter the underbody and also examine closely the adjacent sill endings. Take a look underneath the car at the floor in this area and at the under-sill area. Next, turn your attention to inside the cockpit and examine the same areas, around the spring box, from above.

Corrosion and crude patching should be more evident here as it will not be covered up by layers of mud or underseal. Look closely too at the almost vertical rear panel and, emptying the boot of some of its contents if necessary, inspect the rear extensions of the chassis rails where they join the boot floor and the rear inner wings. Back inside the cockpit again, the whole of the floor area should be inspected with the greatest care — one well known motoring magazine bought a 'Frogeye' with what was believed to be a sound floor only to find that it had been completely coated in fibreglass and that underneath it was rotten. It's easily done ....

The area of the car which attracts the tin worm most of all is at the base of the door pillars. Here silt is allowed to lodge which holds in moisture, causing the pillar itself to rot where it adjoins the sill top and leaving that "It came off in me 'and, Sir!" feeling when the bottom door pillar breaks away, leaving the door flapping like a sail. If it looks sound, check it with a magnet to make sure that you are looking at steel plate and not useless plastic filler. Similarly, check the rear wheel arches, another favourite spot for rust and for the filler sculptor to practise his art, while the leading corners of the bonnet, the bottoms of the doors and the beading at the tops of front and back wings can be similarly afflicted. If the beading has to be replaced, the wing to inner panel joint has to be split (the spot welds have to be drilled out) and new beading fitted before the whole thing is welded up again — not exactly a Saturday morning job!

Under the bonnet, check the inner mudguards for rusting at their seams. The engine and front suspension are supported by box section extensions; these are rarely a source of trouble but if kinked could indicate accident damage. The bulkhead itself rarely gives trouble except under the rain channelling at the top which can

sometimes rot and battery acid can sometimes damage the battery tray. The engine itself has no particular weaknesses but listen carefully for timing chain noise, which is not especially expensive or difficult to repair but is indicative of a fairly high mileage, and look inside the oil filler cap where yellow slime or foaming can indicate fairly severe bore and/or valve guide wear. Look, too, inside the radiator cap where signs of oiliness will indicate head gasket problems or even a warped cylinder head. Popping back on the over-run is indicative of one of the A-series engine's most common faults — burned exhaust valves, while basics such as checking for crank rumble and oil being burned through the exhaust should not be missed. Rear axle differentials are prone to whining and clonking and yet can continue to give good service for year after year. Rear brakes are highly prone to seizure unless lubricated at service intervals with brake grease; something which no one ever seems to do. A poor handbrake will probably indicate that they have seized up. Original gearboxes were probably the car's weakest point. If the correct gearbox is fitted, that may be considered a bonus in itself; it will be almost miraculous if first gear is not noisy and if there is very much synchromesh on second gear. A gearbox rebuild in Britain could be expected to cost around the price of four new tyres.

The car's front suspension is excellent in every respect but one. The kingpin is cotter-pinned on to a threaded pin which goes through the wishbone 'eye'. This threaded pin has a habit of turning and working its way into the wishbone metal itself, or seizing. It is sometimes possible to have the wishbone rebushed but the usual remedy is to replace the whole wishbone. Check for regular greasing in this area, which makes the problem less likely to occur. The rear suspension is usually free, apart from the dreaded rust bug in the surrounding areas already mentioned but it is worth checking that the radius arms, which run parallel to the springs have not also rotted out since they can be difficult to renew.

As a general piece of advice, it is probably best to buy a car from one end or other of the extremes of condition. Either a restored car costing a lot of money, or a rough one in need of restoration and which will need money spending on it but which will be restored to known standards, is preferable to a medium priced, medium condition, car which will invariably be a lot worse that was at first feared when examined closely and especially when dismantling begins. Buy wisely and enjoy driving one of the most characterful little cars ever built!

CLUBS, SPECIALISTS & BOOKS

Of course, a good deal of the 'Frogeye's' attractiveness comes from the pleasure it gives to the person sitting in the driver's seat. But the lone pleasures of owning, maintaining, restoring and driving a 'Frogeye' are multiplied several times over when those pleasures and the experiences of them can be shared with others and when a little more can be learned about the car. The best way of meeting like-minded enthusiasts is by joining the appropriate one-make club which provides meetings, competitions and shows for the enthusiast to attend and which is the best source of all for practical, down to earth information on running the car. And not only will there be social and practical benefits from 'joining the club', there will probably be financial ones, too, saving the membership fee several times over.

Clubs, services and books are detailed in the following list with, after each one, a brief resume of what it has to offer. There are, of course, others but those shown below are those which are most well known and which, in the author's opinion, have most to offer the Mk I Sprite owner.

Clubs

To join the **Austin-Healey Club**
send an sae to Ms Carol Marks, 171 Coldharbour Rd., Bristol BS6 7SX, England. The Club is also split into various area registers within the UK. Local Centre Secretaries' names and addresses are:

Midlands: Mel Knight, 17, Glebe Road, Groby, Leics.
Eastern: David Hicks, 102, Fairfax Drive, Westcliffe-on-Sea, Essex.
New Forest: Mrs Pat Martin, 104, Winchester Road, Shirley, Southampton, Hants.
Northern: Mrs Sheila Reich, 61, Winstanley Road, Sale, Cheshire.
South Western: Mrs Carol Marks, 171, Coldharbour Road, Bristol BS6 7SX
Southern Counties: Phil Young, Mole End, Wallcrouch, Wadhurst, Sussex.
Thames Valley: Tom Oakman, 14, Burnt Oak, Wokingham, Berks.

Overseas Clubs
United States Austin-Healey Club of America, c/o Richard Neville, 21 Allen Lane, Ipswich Ma. 01938, USA.
Canada: Ken Barrow, MPO Box 2293, Calgary, Alberta T 2P 2MS, Canada.
Austin-Healey Owners Association of British Columbia,: PO Box 80274, South Burnaby, B.C. V5H 3X5, Canada.
New Zealand: New Zealand AHC, PO Box 25-016, St Helier, Auckland 5, New Zealand.
Sweden: A-H.C. of Sweden, Box 8142, 16321 Sparga, Sweden.
France: Austin-Healey Club France, Denis Clause, 17 Rue de Port Royal, 10470 St. Lambert, France.
Holland: Austin-Healey Owners' Club Nederland, J.P. Broers, De Gondel 15, Baam, Holland.
Australia: AHOC of Queensland, Carl Stecher, 17 Morhead Avenue, Norman Park Australia 4170. **AHC or West Australia,** Mike Griffiths, 26 Yanagin Crescent, City Beach, W. Australia. **South Australia AHOC,** c/o John Read, 24 Monalta Drive, Belair, S. A. 5052.
Branch AHOC, Ed Jensz, 62 Wales Street, Footscray, Victoria, Australia. **AHOC of Victoria,** c/o Jim McConville, Thermal Heat Treatment Pty. Ltd., 32, First Avenue, Sunshine, Victoria 3020. **AHC of Western Australia,** PO Box 70, Maylands, W.A. 6051.

Specialists

University Motors (USA): Prop: John H. Twist. Mail order service, excellent technical know-how, full workshop facilities. University Motors Ltd., 614, Eastern Avenue S.E., Grand Rapids, Michigan, 49503, U.S.A.
Spridgebits Ltd. Props: Grahame Sykes and Jed Watts. 'Spridget' specialists, as their name suggests. Carry a wide range of spares including a vast range of 'Frogeye' repair panels, upholstery and mechanical parts as well as exchange, reconditioned bodyshells. Full workshop facilities. Nothing too much trouble! Spridgebits Ltd. (Mailing Address), 54, Saint Peters Road, Handsworth, Birmingham B20, England (Telephone 021-554-2033).
Austin-Healey Spares Ltd. Prop: Fred Draper, once Healey Car Co. Storeman. Courteous and friendly. A-H Spares Ltd., Unit 7, Westfield Road, Southam Industrial Estate, Southam, Warwickshire CV33 0JH, England. (Telephone 0926-817181).
The Classic Restoration Centre. The Author's own bodyshop, specialising in 'Frogeye' and other 'Spridget' restorations to a high standard. The Classic Restoration Centre, Lea Lane, Upper Sapey, Worcester, England. (Telephone 088 67 695).
Lifesure Ltd. Specialists in providing car insurance for classic cars of all types, especially for Agreed Value policies where the car's value is agreed in advance rather then left to the low 'book' values that normally prevail. Lifesure Ltd., 34, New Street, St

Neots, Huntingdon, Cambs PE19 1NQ, England. (Telephone 0480-74604/75148).

Books

Sprites and Midgets – Guide to Purchase and Restoration, by Lindsay Porter. Gives a clear and thorough guide to every aspect of buying, running and restoration including all bodywork repairs, of every model of Sprite and Midget. Published by Haynes/G.T. Foulis in 1983.

More Healeys, by Geoffrey Healey. The genuine inside story of 'Frogeye' development and production. Strong on fact and anecdote and easy to read. Published by Gentry Books, London.

The Sprites and Midgets, by Eric Dymock. Concise guide in the ''Collector's Guide'' series. Usual sense of *deja vu* Published by Motor Racing Publications.

M.G. Midget & A-H Sprite Owner's Workshop Manual. A complete guide to all mechanical repairs to all models. Published by Haynes.

PHOTO GALLERY

1. The distinctive appearance of a 'Frogeye' is something quite unique. Protruding headlamps were not so much designed into the car, as forced upon the manufacturers by American headlamp height regulations and by the high cost of fitting a retracting headlamp system. Front bumper and over-riders were optional extras when new but the headlamp stone guards and wing mounted mirrors are later additions.

2

4

3

2. Perhaps the nearest thing to a competitor for the 'Frogeye' at the time of its launch was the fibreglass Berkeley with several innovative features. Unfortunately it also had a very poor reliability record.

3. An early 'Frogeye' is seen parked at Abingdon in the presence of a tribe of 'Big' Healeys, watching in the background. Note the poor bonnet/sill fit. Perhaps modern restorers shouldn't despair! (Courtesy B.L. Heritage)

4. Early prototype Sprites had external hinges but these were replaced by the simple concealed type shown here well before production began.

5

6

7

5. Front suspension was straight from the Austin A30/A35. The drum brake looks really tiny by modern standards but the car was so light that the brakes coped well with everyday driving. (Courtesy Paul Skilleter)

6. The under-bonnet area was a collection of Austin and some Nuffield components. Access to everything but the battery was superb. (Courtesy Paul Skilleter)

7. Destined for the U.S. market in all probability, this early Sprite shows the ribbed rubber floor covering now all but extinct as most have been replaced by carpet. (Courtesy B.L. Heritage)

8
9
10
11

8. From the rear quarters, the rounded shape of the front end can be seen to balance and complement the curves of the car's rear. The absence of a boot lid was part of a deliberate policy on the part of the Healey designers to save weight and at the same time maximise body shell strength; the Frogeye was, after all, the first monocoque sports car and therefore a bit of an unknown quantity in that respect.

9. On the very earliest cars, the hood was fitted to the screen by a row of nine lift-the-dot fasteners. This was far from watertight and was quickly superseded by a system which had been used on earlier Warwick-built Healeys. The screen frame was designed to be quickly detachable with just two screws each side.

10. The very earliest cars had triangulated box-section

fillets reinforcing the rear inner wing/boot floor joint. Later cars had a complete curved front to rear box-section 'chassis' member in its place.

11. A method of identifying the earliest Sprites is by the shape of the windscreen frame stanchion which is of squarer section than those on the later cars.

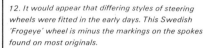

12

13

12. It would appear that differing styles of steering wheels were fitted in the early days. This Swedish 'Frogeye' wheel is minus the markings on the spokes found on most originals.

13. Very few cars remain nowadays that have not been **totally restored at least once (and usually several times)** during their lifetime. The car's distinctive appearance and obvious character make the process most worthwhile.

14. Jacking was designed to be simple, a single tube situated behind the outer sill but fixed to the inner sill and the inside of the centre crossmember above the floor, took the weight.

15. Tucked away beneath the plug leads, the car's unusual tachometer drive take-off is situated. Lucas and Smiths collaborated over this ingenious solution to a difficult problem.

14

15

16

17

18

19

20

21

16. Road testers frequently criticised the early Sprite for having pedals which were too closely grouped and indeed they do look a bit on the cramped side!

17. Another frequent source of criticism was the boot which was voluminous enough, but could be a real pain if the spare wheel had to be removed and an even bigger pain if the deflated tyre was wet and dirty and had to be pushed in alongside luggage.

18. The Austin A35 gearbox extension was fitted with a turret at the end of its remote gearchange. The Sprite's gearbox tunnel was given a steel box to fit around this turret.

19. When a car radio was fitted it was placed where the grab handle had been. Many Sprite grab handles have been removed in the intervening years for far less 'pure' reasons!

20. The earliest type of sidescreen was a relatively flimsy, one-piece affair of which hardly any examples still survive. Later types were of different shapes and sizes according to whether the car was fitted with a hardtop or not.

21. The weighty bonnet is held open by a pair of telescopic supports — one on each side.

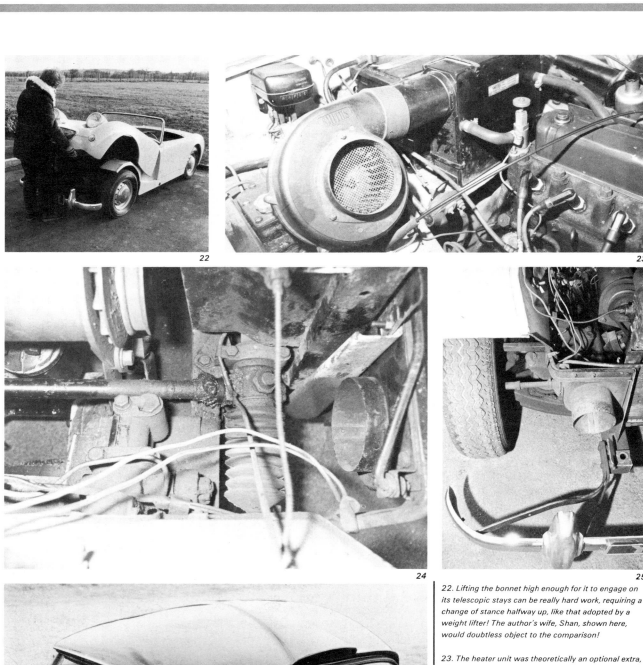

22

23

24

25

26

22. *Lifting the bonnet high enough for it to engage on its telescopic stays can be really hard work, requiring a change of stance halfway up, like that adopted by a weight lifter! The author's wife, Shan, shown here, would doubtless object to the comparison!*

23. *The heater unit was theoretically an optional extra, although there are hardly any cars without one fitted. Missing from this heater is the length of trunking which runs to the front of the car where it collects forced-in fresh air when the car is on the move.*

24. *Down beneath the wires and cables, ahead of the axle line, lurks the Morris Minor steering rack which is responsible for the Sprite's super-sensitive steering.*

25. *Well ahead of the front chassis outriggers is the front bumper and its support brackets. Bumpers could save the bonnet from expensive parking damage and were an optional extra well worth having.*

26. *Many different styles of hardtop were available, sold in competition with the official works offering. This one, from Pride & Clarke in London (but sold nationally by mail order), was one of the most popular and distinctive.*

27. Less well-known, and now extremely rare, are these exterior door handles available in the early Sixties as aftermarket accessories.

28. "How on earth am I going to get in there?" Access was always slightly cramped but not that *difficult*, surely?

29. Hoods are removed by first taking the tension out of the hood frame and then unclipping it from the top of the windscreen.

30. With all the lift-the-dot fasteners undone, the hood is then pulled back off the two rear body clips.

31. It is then simply lifted off the hood rails before being folded up ...

27

28

29

30

31

32. ... and placed carefully in the pothole that passes for a boot!

33. Last of all, the one-piece hood frame is folded, reversed, and placed into the two holes waiting for it behind the seats and near the floor.

34. Increasing numbers of 'Frogeyes' are being restored to high standards. This one is barely recognisable as a 'Frog' but in any case, with wrong wheels, engine, gearbox and a fibreglass bonnet complementing an amazingly rusty shell, the car was fit only for the spares that remained.

35. An important consideration in a car being bought for restoration is the condition of the seats, which can be expensive to repair properly even though they are not leather.

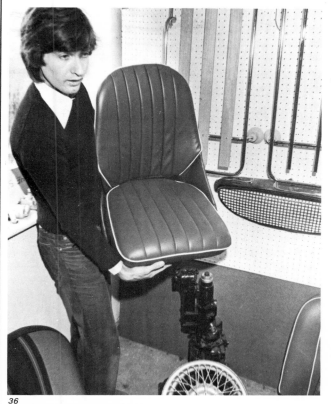

36

37

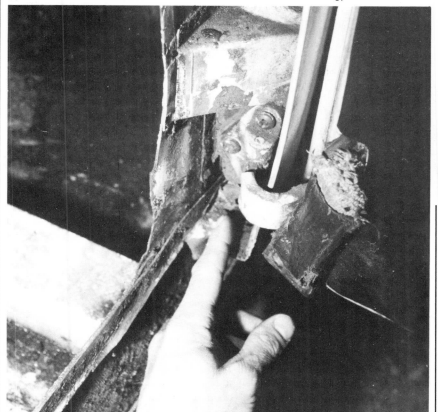

39

38

36. Grahame Sykes, of Spridgebits, holds one of their re-covered seats, which are available on an exchange basis provided that the old seat bases are in good condition.

37. Even more important, of course, is the condition of the bodyshell. Here the rear floor/spring box area has rotted almost to the point of no return, although anything can be repaired if enough funds are available!

38. The author's own bodyshop handles more Sprites than any other car and finds that another favourite rot-spot (and one which is frequently worse than it seems at first) is the door hinge pillar in this area.

39. Steel bonnets fetch a premium nowadays and even those which have rusted badly in these typical areas are well worth saving using the repair panels supplied by people like Spridgebits.

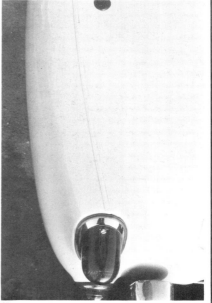

40. Boot floor, where it curves up over the petrol tank, and the rear apron, are also prone to the ravages of the rust bug.

41. This is the rear wing shown from above where the beading strip can clearly be seen. To replace this properly requires the removal of the whole rear wing — an expensive affair, needless to say.

42. An original looking dashboard can be a strong selling point and original steering wheels are also highly prized. Most cars have been fitted with non-standard wheels at some time in their lives, like this one.

43. Correct ventilated wheels, correct hubcaps; easily taken for granted but essential from the point of view of originality.

44. This bonnet stay, used for supplementing the telescopic stays during a windy day, is something which is frequently missing on a car offered for sale.

45

46

47

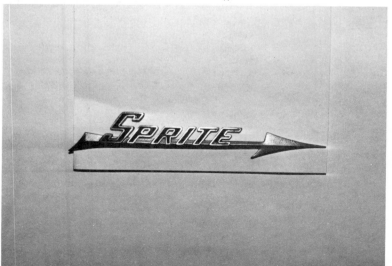

48

45. Bonnet catches, when still fitted, are rarely as smart as this one. Note the crude, but correct, springing system.

46. The correct rear view mirror; a humble item, but where would you find one if it was missing from a car you bought?

47. Correct carburettors are these 'brass topped' $1\frac{1}{8}$ inch HS1 S.U.s. So often, the later and much more common $1\frac{1}{4}$ inch HS2 carburettors have been fitted in their place.

48. Badges are something that can be renewed, thanks to the availability of high-quality replacement badges now being manufactured again.

49

50

51

52

53

54

49. Front inner wings are constructed from flat pieces of steel, but even they rot out. Replacements can be bought or quite simply made but, again, the time and expense of getting everything absolutely right is usually greater than the extra cost of buying an original, complete car in the first place.

50. The author's own 'Frogeye', bought as an uncompleted restoration project. The advantages of buying this way are that the cost is usually very much lower and that the very worst can usually be seen right at the start.

51. The 'Frogeye' was the only Sprite to use a round Sprite badge. Later badges, used on the Mk II and later models, were of the winged variety and lost the coat of arms.

52. From a higher angle, the headlamps look less obtrusive and the overall roundness of the shape is evident.

53. From lower down, the hood irons and headlamp nacelles give a more 'gawky' appearance – the car almost looks ready to spring forward, frog-like.

54. Sprites, like this example, are sometimes fitted with amber flasher lenses from the Morris Minor Traveller (and others) but standard white flashers are quite legal on cars of this age in the UK.

55

56

57

58

55. It is interesting to note how close in appearance are this very early car (Courtesy B.L. Heritage) ...

56. ... and this much later car.

57. Like most successful things, Sprites are simple, uncluttered, easy to maintain and very appealing!

58. Perhaps the 'Frogeye's' chances of survival have been higher than most. With as pleasing a profile as this, its future is almost guaranteed.

59. From above, the thing that strikes you most is the car's size – or lack of it. You almost feel as if James Willis, this car's owner, could reach out and touch both ends.

60. With the doors open, the fact that the car consists of a front and rear held together only by strength in the floorpan and sills becomes obvious.

59

60

61

62

63

64

61. On a bright day, even with the leaves gone from the trees, the urge to take the top down will be well nigh irresistible!

62. Although later Sprites and Midgets were obviously different, they were also not-so-obviously similar in many areas. The 'Frogeye's' sill structure, seen here, was almost exactly the same as that used on the last M.G. Midget, built over twenty years later.

63. When replacement time came, Healeys were responsible for redesigning the shape of the front end. This is a hybrid prototype still with the 'Frogeye' rear end. (Courtesy B.L. Heritage) ...

64. ... the final result – the now rare Austin-Healey Sprite Mk II with 948cc engine. Note the MGB-look-alike, Abingdon-designed rear end.

65. 'Frogeyes' have always been competed as fun cars, rather than as out-and-out winners. Here Chris Marks of the Austin-Healey Owners Club is seen at Prescott. (Courtesy Phil Beevers).

65

66. James Thacker (135) in his ex-Alec Poole 1150cc car awaits the start of his first race at the M.G. Car Club's 1971 Brands Hatch meeting. Alongside is Charles Merriman in his ex-Alan Woodie 1150 Sprite ...

66

67. ... Six years on and James Thacker is seen again in the May 1977 M.G.C.C. Silverstone event.

68. The end of the Frogeye Sprite. Except that, more than two decades after the last one left the factory, they are now more sought after than ever.

C1

C2

C3

C1 "The car that offers so much – for so little", reproduced from a very early sales brochure. Note the one-piece, flimsy plastic sidescreens which are now extremely rare, having been discontinued at an early stage. Those originally fitted were usually replaced by the later type as they became tatty.

C2 Reverse of the same brochure. The somewhat mature gentleman in the sales brochure's cover picture turned out to be not the sort of person eventually identified with the 'Frogeye'.

C3 Before the days of Austin-Healey, Donald Healey had been responsible for a number of other models. This early Warwick-built Healey is typical of his Riley-engined sporting cars.

C4 This cherry red Sprite, 255 JPH, is the actual car given away by Practical Classics as the prize in their first, and amazingly successful, "Win a Classic Car competition" ...

C5 ... The car was painstakingly restored for the magazine by Terry Bramall. Not only is the dashboard of this car almost original it is also fitted with the correct steering wheel, examples of which are in particularly short supply. Note how pronounced are the 'frogeyes' from the drivers viewpoint!

C6 The friendly face of the Sprite. Despite the fishy number plate of this car, this view illustrates well why the model acquired its nicknames of 'frogeye' and 'bugeye'. The 'racing' mirrors and headlamp grilles lend a period feel, even though the mirrors are not really contemporary.

C4

C5

C6

C7, C8 & C9 Three views showing the simple, unadorned lines of the original Sprite. Despite this simplicity the 'Frogeye' oozes character and is still enormous fun to drive, even though, by today's standards, it has a very modest performance.

C7

C8

C9

C10

C11

C10 'Frogeye' doors were as bare as could be imagined, but at least gave some storage room, some elbow room and sidescreens which did not allow rust-creating water into the door shells. Note that the base of the door pillar is often seriously affected by rust.

C11 Close-up showing the arrangement of rear lights and bumpers. The arrowed, "Sprite" badge is the correct original fitting. Of course there is no external access to the boot!

C12 Open wide! The Sprite's one-piece bonnet when open gives terrific access to the faithful and reliable Austin A-series-derived engine and its ancillary components. Prone to serious rusting in the area of the sidelights, many original all-steel bonnets have been discarded over the years to be replaced by fibreglass substitutes – this makes steel bonnets in good condition extremely valuable.

C12

C13 & 14 *Replacement bonnets in fibreglass did not necessarily resemble the original steel components as these two examples show. Often they were modelled on the lines of more exotic sports cars to give the Sprite a 'racier' appearance.*

C13

C14

C15 The Sprite that followed the 'Frogeye' had a totally re-designed front end and other major body panels, but under the totally changed skin, the Sprite Mk II was almost exactly the same including mechanics and chassis-cum-floorpan.

C16 The original 'Frogeye' spawned a whole family of 'Spridgets' (Sprites/Midgets) which would serve the needs of sports car enthusiasts throughout the world for many years after production of the original ceased. Although these later cars brought improvements in comfort and performance, none recaptured the character and raw appeal of the 'Frogeye'.

C15

C16

C17

C18

C17 & C18 Another way to enjoy the Sprite – Trials (or 'Mud-plugging'). Although the ground clearance of this car has been modified to make it more competitive it still retains its shapely charm and, judging by their grins, the owners are having fun!

C19 This car, in action at Donington, is reputed to be an ex-works Sprite (Chris Harvey)

C20 Brighton Speed Trials was the setting for this 'Frogeye' wearing wire wheels and stopped by front disc brakes – the original drum brakes are known to be highly prone to fade in sporting events. (Chris Harvey)

C19

C20